praise for
nicotine

"A satisfying wisp of an essay about tobacco, addiction, first cigarettes, last cigarettes, breathing, kissing, hypnosis, literature, memory, and marking time... *Nicotine* is a smoke ring, blown perfectly in a single puff, or—better?—a wafting trail of vapor." —*Harper's*

"Cigarettes function as punctuation for life, argues Gregor Hens...They make it coherent and add drama, inserting commas, semicolons, and ellipses (and, in the end, an inarguable and often premature full stop). Smoking is bad for you, but that doesn't mean it can't be fun."
— *The Economist,* Books of the Year

"A slim but plaintive memoria to a lost love—a philosophical meditation on the nature of addiction, the listlessness, the frustration, and the sense of grief one feels at the loss of a fix. Its structure is reminiscent of the memoryscapes of W. G. Sebald...This intelligent, literary volume plumbs Mark Twain, Italo Svevo, and Van Morrison. But make no mistake: *Nicotine* isn't a self-help book. It's not an anti-smoking screed. Nor is it a love sonnet to tobacco. It's an honest exposition of the emotional complexity of quitting." —*Washington Post*

"If *Nicotine* has a literary progenitor I would say that it is *In Search of Lost Time*, in which Proust made the material of seven volumes bloom out of one French cookie dunked in a cup of tea... Hens uses a similar alchemy to transform the things of his world — the family in which he grew up, in Cologne; his former home in Columbus, where he taught German literature at Ohio State; his apartment in Berlin, where he lives with his wife, and produces novels and translations—into whole relay stations of poetic force, humming and sparking and chugging...an extraordinary act of literary finesse... his story becomes captivating—laced with a saving irony—by being told through the medium of something as humble as tobacco... [a] dark, lovely, funny book." —*The New Yorker*

"Part memoir, part philosophical lament...dry, earthy, and combustible, like a Virginia tobacco blend, [*Nicotine*] has a lot to say and says it well... Like any author worth reading, Mr. Hens is sometimes best when he goes off-topic... His lapidary prose will sometimes put you in mind of the chain-smoking Norwegian writer Karl Ove Knausgaard's." —*New York Times*

"*Nicotine* is not another finger-wagging treatise on the evils of smoking. Nor is it a boring, triumphant tale of how one can muster the willpower to dump the cigarettes and replace them with a diet of unpasteurized goat's milk and raw parsnips... Instead this is a wonderfully meandering

memoir, beautifully written, in which Mr. Hens recalls formative experiences through the experience of smoking—because cigarettes were always present—while also exploring the psychology of an addict."
— *Wall Street Journal*

"*Nicotine* is a serious investigation. Hens's memories—spun as stories, for he is a piquant, enchanting storyteller—follow one after another, though not before they have been surgically dissected for elements of self-discovery lurking in that memory's cigarette. Will Self's introduction is a gloriously mad prelude...Despite qualms that the last cigarette might extinguish his access to literarily fertile material, *Nicotine* is proof positive that Hens still has the stuff." —*San Francisco Chronicle*

"Readers and smokers and especially readers who smoke will be grateful that Mr. Hens wrote *Nicotine* despite the risk of relapse. It is that rare book on addiction: neither preaching nor self-loathing, lapsing only occasionally into romanticism. And like the best cigarettes, it is over too soon." —*The Economist*

"There are too many books, essays, movies, and songs about cigarettes. But *Nicotine* somehow manages to feel fresh in spite of that. Ultimately, it's a book about longing, and you don't need to be a current or former smoker to relate to that." —*New York Magazine*

"[An] excellent personal work on the fetishization, the ceremony, and the compulsions of the smoker... *Nicotine* is a meandering journey through a life of everyday addiction, soaked in memories stained sepia by tobacco smoke... The writing is superb, an unclassifiable mix of freeform thought and transcribed memory, reminiscent of the wonderful essayist Geoff Dyer. Its malleable structure, through sheer skill and confidence, allow the many digressions to remain ever valid and precise." —*The Skinny*

"An idiosyncratic and thought-provoking essay... Hens gives readers an understanding of what it is like to have an addiction, albeit a legal one, and how the end of an addiction can be felt as a loss." —*Publishers Weekly*

"[An] unorthodox and candid memoir... [Hens] is an idiosyncratic stylist whose sentences are often terse and elliptical, and Calleja's translation ably captures his unique voice. In a book that is as much a paean to smoking as it is a eulogy, Hens is both poetic and unforgiving about the pleasures and pains of smoking." —*Kirkus Reviews*

"The writing is detailed, fluid, and sensual. The acute memories [Hens] shares about people who have crossed his path are especially appealing... Smoking and cigarettes might not be good for the health of the body, but Hens's glimpse through the prism of addiction offers an enriching and enlightening account that benefits the mind and the soul." —*Shelf Awareness*

NICO-
TINE a love story up in smoke

gregor hens

translated from the German by
Jen Calleja

with an introduction by
Will Self

OTHER PRESS
NEW YORK

First softcover edition 2021
ISBN 978-1-63542-052-4

Copyright © Gregor Hens, 2011
Originally published in Germany by S. Fischer Verlag in 2011

Translation copyright © Jen Calleja, 2015
First English edition published in Great Britain
by Fitzcarraldo Editions in 2015

Production editor: Yvonne E. Cárdenas
Text designer: Julie Fry

This book was set in Baskerville and DIN.

10 9 8 7 6 5 4 3 2 1

Library of Congress Cataloging-in-Publication Data

Names: Hens, Gregor, 1965– , author. | Calleja, Jen, translator.
Title: Nicotine / by Gregor Hens ; translated from the German
    by Jen Calleja ; with an introduction by Will Self.
Other titles: Nikotin. English
Description: New York : Other Press, 2016.
Identifiers: LCCN 2015050047 | ISBN 9781590517932
    (hardcover) | ISBN 9781590517949 (e-book)
Subjects: LCSH: Hens, Gregor, 1965– | Authors, German—
    20th century—Biography. | Authors, German—21st
    century—Biography. | Smoking.
Classification: LCC PT2708.E5 Z46 2016 | DDC 838/.9209–dc23
LC record available at http://lccn.loc.gov/2015050047

Negating an act is somehow similar to changing the direction of a moving body. A break, a zero velocity, is necessary in between switching from one to the other.

—Moshe Feldenkrais

introduction

It happens all the time—how could it not, since
the very repetitive nature of the habit calls it forth?
In response to my deployment of one or another of
my nicotine delivery systems, an interlocutor will
ask after my dependency, and so I'll begin talking
about some aspect of it—but after a few seconds
I'll pause, with a catch in my throat not unlike the
epiglottal spasm that precedes a tobacco-induced
coughing fit. At these times I can feel it all banking
up inside me: a great twisted mass of tics, compulsions, culturally transmitted attitudes, complexes,
and neuroses. Swooning, I picture the baroque
façade of my forty-year relationship with La Diva
Nicotina—its myriad niches and grottos (each
one suitable for a swift fag break), its blue-faced
gargoyles and hand-rolled finials that rise up, row
upon foil-wrapped row, to where an upended *belli-
coso* cigar of a spire chars the heavens. How, I ask

myself, how can I possibly convey to this person — for all that he may have smoked himself, may indeed be still smoking — the all-pervading nature of my addiction to this psychoactive substance, which has tangled up my psyche in its writhing convolvulus of highs and lows, even as it's toxified every cell in my body? The answer of course is, I can't. And so after a few desultory remarks about whatever smoking-cessation therapy I'm currently engaged in, I'll usually nudge the conversation in the direction of clearer skies.

The other evening, cycling across the small park surrounding the Imperial War Museum (formerly the lunatic asylum known as Bedlam), I was hailed by a passerby who recognized me. "How's it going with the vape, Will?" he called out, and since I'd just finished smoking a cigarette and contemplating my grim new addictive dispensation, I stopped to tell him, "Dreadful. My wife gave me the vape for Christmas, and rather ironically — since I'd just managed to pack in smoking, although I was still chewing nicotine gum — I found myself more heavily addicted to nicotine than ever after twenty-four hours of suckling compulsively on this!" I withdrew my silvery, top-of-the-range vaporizer from my pocket. "Which is why I call it 'the witch's tit.'" The man was bemused — he'd only wanted a glancing acknowledgment, not the prologue to a lecture, which then continued, "I tell you, I became so fixated on this bloody thing it didn't take long before I began casting surreptitious glances at cigarettes and wondering whether smoking might constitute an effective substitute for vaping. Now I'm doing both! I'm nailed up on a crucifix the upright of which is a vaporizer, while the crossbar is a Gitanes—*sans filtre, bien sûr*..."

Ah! Gitanes, with their elegant blue flat pack, adorned with a Carmen-like silhouette of a full–skirted woman seemingly dancing the tarantella in a cloud of their own smoke. I could've expatiated to the man at length simply on my relationship with French tobacco—beginning with the origins of the state monopoly in the strong black shag issued to the Grande Armée, and dubbed "*le petit gris*" after the color of the cubic paper packets it was wrapped in (and still is two centuries later). I could've painted him a picture: the pale sable dust of a village square somewhere in the Midi shaded by planes and chestnuts; the café-bar-cum-*tabac* with its zinc counter and scowling patron; the *grand noir* and a small balloon of Marc de Bourgogne; the just purchased packet of Boyards Maïs and its reverent unwrapping: silky cellophane slipped off, cardboard lappet unlimbered, and the thick cigarette in its yellowy binding of maize paper eased out. The coffee, brandy, and tobacco are so inextricably bound up with one another—and with those overnight drives I regularly undertook in my twenties, beginning in London and ending in Provence—that I cannot catch a whiff of the French stuff without hearing the ghostly chinking of boules and the mechanical flutteration of a two-horsepower engine.

And this would've been merely a prologue-within-a-prologue: Had the man in the madding park displayed the least inclination, I'd have gone on—detailing exhaustively my relations not only with French tobacco but also those I've cultivated with the weed of many other nations as well. I shan't overshare here when a few vignettes should suffice. For the past decade or so, I've often agreed to give lectures and readings in Berlin solely so I can visit the tobacconist in the Alexanderplatz Bahnhof. Here I buy hand-rolling cigarette tobaccos of a stygian darkness and Samsonian strength unattainable in England—my favorite is the threatening-sounding Schwarzer Krauser № 1. It's the same with Italy, which I visit not for the astonishing Mannerist frescoes of Modena's Palazzo del Te but for its pleasingly cheap and tasty eponymous cheroots as well. Cuba, alas, is too far a-*finca* for me, but for a number of years I had a cigar dealer who'd arrive at my house with a Gladstone bag full of Havanas—including so-called specials, which, as their name implies, were accorded the very best ever to be rolled, and superior to the established *marques*. As with all illicit dealers (he transshipped the cigars through Estonia and smuggled them from there into England, thus avoiding the hefty customs duty), I felt under an obligation to smoke enough to justify his risks. Ridiculous, I know—but that's how I ended up with a £15 per day Hoyo de Monterrey Petit Robusto habit on top of the cigarettes.

The first cigarettes I ever smoked were bone-dry Senior Service that had long lurked in one of the silver cigarette boxes scattered about my grand-parents' house. Certainly I was nauseated—I may even have vomited—but this is all lost in the blue–gray curlicues of the past. By the time I was at secondary school, and walking a couple of miles there each morning, I was a confirmed smoker who'd stop off in the park for an 8:00 a.m. fag break. As the advertising slogan of the period put it, "People Like You Are Changing..." The agent of change being a harsh and wood-smoky Player's N$^{\underline{o}}$6 or its still harsher and wood-smokier, scaled-down stablemate: a N$^{\underline{o}}$10. In funds, I smoked Peter Stuyvesants in the soft pack, or Kensitas in a red flip-top box. I never liked Embassy much—the smoke felt oddly "woolly" in my mouth—but had a thing for old men's filterless fags: Navy Cut, Woodbine, and Park

Drive. Soon enough, as my smoking increased, I sought out cheaper whiffs—settling on half ounces of Old Holborn tobacco, each of which could be concocted into nearly thirty whippet-thin roll-ups.

Even age thirteen, I was hip to the powerful ways smoking could alter my perception. Certainly nicotine was psychoactive—it transported me in paradoxical ways, tugging my feelings about in its choppy wake. The first few drags after a period of abstinence induced head spin and dry mouth, while a drowsy numbness crept over my extremities. Soon enough, though, this narcotic phase was succeeded by excitation: spit balled in my mouth, my palms itched, my heartbeat accelerated—in my own small and unsophisticated way, staring at the algal scurf on the duck pond, I believed I could *achieve something*. Really, the narcotic effects of nicotine—since they're so paradoxically up and down—are best understood by analogy: It's the lightweight and socially integrated version of Dexamyl, better known by its slang name: purple heart. The agents of the first real drug craze to hit Britain, purple hearts were the original mother's little helpers: a combination of speed and barbiturate that calmed you down even as they zizzed you up. Of course, any parabola reaches its zenith—or its nadir—but the appeal of purple hearts or nicotine is that up and down cancel each other out, which is why those who use them simply keep on going. For a while.

This glowing ember of awareness came cupped in a gestural hand. True, by the early 1970s, those who were truly hip to the zeitgeist were packing the habit in. Some had beaten government legislation to the punch. I once asked my friend the writer and former gangster John McVicar when he stopped smoking, and without pausing to draw breath he snapped, "I read the so-called doctors' study linking smoking and lung cancer when it was popularized in the mid-fifties. I stopped immediately." This is the behavior of a true man of action: Having received a reliable reconnaissance report of trouble ahead, he immediately changes his line of advance. My own mother, although disqualified by sex from the epithet, nonetheless had her own moment of clarity—the sight of my grandfather dying of lung cancer—and so took action. She expeditiously canned her forty-a-day habit—although medical research would suggest it was already too late for me, age three, who'd been sucking on the witch's tit more or less continually since conception. It was too late for her as well: The crab took her at age sixty-four. So messages were mixed when I was in my nicotinic infancy: On the one hand, cigarette advertising on British television was already banned (although not cigars—

a cognitive dissonance personified by a Hamlet panatela smoldering to the strains of J. S. Bach's "Air on the G String"); yet between the truncated fingers of another hand—one belonging to the Irish comedian Dave Allen—a fag merrily combusted on TV at prime time each Saturday evening. At school, if we wanted to smoke, we went to the little park by the library across the road. Until we were in the lower sixth form, that is—because, of course, smoking was allowed in our common room.

As soon as I could get away with smoking in the street, I acquired a fedora, angled its brim, and struck Bogartian attitudes while glimpsing my reflection in shop windows. I also stared with forthright narcissism at my neotenous smoking self in the windows of tube and train carriages—and surely nothing summons up the once solid social structure of mass smoking than this phenomenon: puffing in transit. I smoked in cars and on buses, I smoked on trains and on planes. I had a cigarette on the tube I took from Caledonian Road to King's Cross on the evening of November 18, 1987, which was pretty cognitively dissonant of me, since I was in one of my fitness phases and en route to a karate class at the dojo on Judd Street. I remember stubbing out the fag on the floor of the smoking carriage—remember because of the way the rubberized grooves always seemed to me purpose-designed to accommodate butts. Remember also, because a scant hour or so after I loped up the Piccadilly Line escalator, a fellow puffer dropped his still smoldering cigarette in the grooves of a tread, and it was carried into the oily, fluffy, highly combustible netherworld. The ensuing fire killed thirty-one, injured a further one hundred, and put a stop to smoking on the London underground forever.

At the risk of making me out to be a sort of Zelig of tobacco — in the wrong place at the right historic time, every time — I was also a passenger on the last scheduled plane flight out of Heathrow on which smoking was permitted. Coincidentally, I'd been awarded an upgrade. So it was that as the 747, en route to New York, broke through the cloud cover, and the first-class cabin was flooded with unearthly light, I lit up. I'd already been given a bottle of champagne to cuddle during takeoff, and as I sipped and sucked, I was fully aware that the entire baroque edifice of socialized nicotine consumption was staggering before my eyes, as a swirl of cigarette smoke released into a car's confines staggers for a split second after you've cracked the window open, before disappearing into the void.

In his superb *Nicotine*, Gregor Hens animadverts on the origins of this oft-quoted sentiment: "I've given up smoking more than any man alive, every time I stub one out I swear it's my last." Hens says it's often misattributed to Mark Twain, but I'd always assumed it was from Italo Svevo's novel *Confessions of Zeno*, which is—among much else—a minatory portrait of the way habit crimps the psyche. When I was writing my own smoke-cured novel, *The Butt*, I went looking for the line to use as an epigraph, but unable to find it had recourse to this one instead: "Who knows, whether, if I had given up smoking, I should really have become the strong perfect man I imagined? Perhaps it was this very doubt that bound me to my vice, because life is so much pleasanter if one is able to believe in one's own latent greatness." Which, frankly, fitted the bill far better, because Svevo grasps the real nettle here: In a culture in which using a particular intoxicant is accorded the status of a quasi-acceptable vice, the individual smoker's self-conception becomes hopelessly divided: On the one virtuous hand there's nary a yellowy stain, while on the other the taint is deep and jaundiced. The problem for the long-term (the deranging expression in English is "committed") smoker is that as public prohibitions have increased and become more egregious, so his notion of "the strong perfect man" he might become if he jacked the sordid business in is rendered increasingly tenebrous—a blue-gray smirch filtering the harsh glare of public health policy.

After all, if tobacco smoking is held to be universally bad, not to do it may be accorded only common sense rather than a virtue.

I gave up smoking in 2000 using Allen Carr's celebrated manual of piety *Easyway to Stop Smoking*. I followed Carr's catechism to the letter, continuing to smoke as I read the short text, and stubbing out my last as I turned the final page. Carr's method is really a sort of proleptic aversion therapy, his point being that smokers are victims of a false consciousness: There's nothing at all pleasant about smoking, and we naïve and immature wannabes were deluded by its social cachet, while simultaneously compelled by physical addiction. According to Carr, given the rapidity with which nicotine is absorbed by the human body, the smoker is almost constantly in a state of withdrawal—and thus mistakes the *relief* of these symptoms for the semblance of pleasure. Schopenhauer, a heavy smoker who fervently believed all pleasure to be merely the cessation of pain, would undoubtedly have approved. I caviled a little at this—hadn't I done everything possible over the years to make my nicotine habit a species of Epicureanism? Was I not the proud possessor of several humidors, scores of briar and meerschaum pipes, cigarette holders, and all sorts of other paraphernalia? (The day I bought a specialized pipe-reaming tool can be accorded either the zenith or the nadir of my habit.) While, as I think I've indicated above, I ceded ground to no one in the breadth and variety of what I was prepared to smoke, when it came to deaccessioning, it took days to empty my tobacco cellar of all its exotica, from Indonesian clove cigarettes to Burmese cheroots via Vietnamese hand-rolling tobacco—and that's just the Southeast Asian section. Carr's typical smoker, by contrast, was a compulsive bottom-feeder, shoveling down machine-rolled filter tip after filter tip, always the same mass-produced brand.

Still, I bought the program and allowed myself to be reconditioned. It was an odd year, the one I went without. As Carr had preached, the physical addiction was easy enough to beat—after three months I barely thought about tobacco at all. I exercised, I felt better if not exactly more virtuous. I was able to write a novel, albeit only a rewrite of Oscar Wilde's one. Of course, when I say I barely thought about tobacco at all, what I mean is I barely thought about *having a fag there and then*. I still thought about tobacco a lot, and in my version of *The Picture of Dorian Gray*—the action of which was brought forward ninety-odd years to the 1980s—the epigram-spouting fop, Henry Wotton, is a deeply committed smoker, his own habit being molded firmly on my own recently abandoned one.

Only when Wotton is actually dying of AIDS does he pack it in—and even then he still manages to aspirate: "*Au fond*, I believe I shall always be smoking." Prophetic words, because who else could my Wotton have been modeled on (besides Wilde's Wotton) but *moi*?

The other incident that, in retrospect, marked the beginning of the end of my life as a nonsmoker occurred on the shores of Lake Wannsee outside Berlin. I was giving a reading at the old DDR Literaturhaus, more or less opposite the villa in which the Final Solution was plotted. The man introducing me was a journalist, a critic, and—more important—a smoker. He was overweight as well, and as he gave his spiel, he sweated and puffed acridity into my smarting eyes. In order to prevent myself from punching the insensitive bastard in his fat self-indulgent face, when the event was over I asked him—in a polite and nonjudgmental way—about his obviously unhealthy lifestyle: the glass after glass of wine he was knocking back, the canapés he was shoveling down, and of course the smoke that plumed from his porcine snout. "It's perfectly simple," he explained. "Almost every morning I wake up feeling like shit and think about packing in my drinking, my eating, and my smoking. But then I remember my grandfather, who was in the Wehrmacht and died at Stalingrad, and I contemplate the terrible suffering and deprivation he must have experienced for months before finally being killed. Surely, I admonish myself, it's up to you to experience all the pleasures he was denied. And then I reach for my cigarettes."

I said at the outset that the very repetitive nature of smoking calls forth anecdotage, but really it's more profound than that. It's the way a smoking habit is constituted by innumerable such little incidents—or "scenes"—strung together along a lifeline, that makes the whole schmozzle so irresistible to the novelist. Gregor Hens believes his very authorial persona was forged in the crucible of his emergent addiction, for on experiencing his first nicotine rush, "I became myself for the very first time." And the sort of self he became was a writerly one: "I not only saw images, not only heard single words or sentences, but also experienced an inner world. I was offered for the first time an experience that was communicable. This is precisely why I can remember this night with such completeness, precisely why I can write it in this form." Hens puts it all down to the drug itself, but for me this is secondary—perhaps because I've taken so many other, more egregious drugs. In my case it's the juxtaposition between a diachronic and an episodic sense of self that smoking affords, which makes it so very hard to let go of. Am I the same person as that child, leaning out the Crittall window of a semi, the smoke from his N⁰ 6 blooming in the suburban night? Or was he somebody else altogether? Every time I spark one up, I'm invited to consider the relationship between all of my smoking selves: Are we a unitary being, or merely disparate characters striking many different attitudes? Am I reborn each time I smoke—a fag-wielding phoenix? Or, like a dormant seed germinated by fire, is there only one essential me, who, *au fond*, will always be smoking?

On the last day of June 2007, I ate with my friend the artist Jon Wealleans at St. John restaurant in Spitalfields. After the plates had been cleared but before the coffee arrived, I offered Jon one of my two remaining Hoyo de Monterrey Petit Robustos. We lit up, and soon a great writhing cloud of smoke swirled about our table. None of the other diners—for all that they weren't smoking themselves—made any objection. The ban on smoking in public buildings in England was still three hours in the future. Nowadays I tell anyone who'll stand still long enough to listen that the increasing prohibitions—legal, social, cultural—on smoking are nothing but a good thing. I barely smoke cigars at all anymore, since the context within which it was pleasing to smoke them has entirely dispersed. My piping is no longer Pan-like since Dunhill stopped selling its superb hand-blended tobaccos. Nor do I smoke many cigarettes, since none of my narcissistic puffing selves likes this image: loitering about by wheelie bins in alleys, whey-faced and vampiric, hanging on to a fag unto grim death. For the past eight years I've more or less rigorously "controlled" my smoking, interpolating scenes from my smoking life with others from my ruminant one. I chew nicotine gum—I even became obsessed enough with snus, the little tea bags of smokeless tobacco you see bulging beneath the lips of Scandinavian TV detectives, to invest in a miniature fridge so I could keep the beastly stuff fresh. I absolutely accept that once the number of nonsmokers exceeds that of smokers, the game—such as it was—is up. What resentment I may feel toward governments that trumpet their public health "victories," even as their economic policies drive thousands into poverty-induced sickness, is emphatically besides the point. In lieu of pursuing my obsession with tobacco, driven on by the hounds of my nicotine addiction, I have focused my energies on this "control," and rolling with Allen Carr and Arthur Schopenhauer, settled for temporary relief in place of true abandonment.

The only thing I want for in this strange liminal realm, in which every time I stub out a cigarette I swear it's my last, is someone to talk to about it—

and not just idly chat, but intensely recall, debate, and rhapsodize my relationship with La Diva Nicotina. The problem is that like the man in the park, they just won't stand for it, having themselves long since packed smoking in, never smoked at all, or are still shamefacedly puffing. Which is why Gregor Hens's essay is such a delight, for here we have a writer who's prepared to indulge his habit in the only way that matters: on the page. Here we have an ex-smoker who absolutely understands that *au fond* he will always be smoking. Moreover, Hens is unafraid to pull the severed horse's head of habituation from the waters of Lethe, and anatomize the eels that writhe from its mouth, nostrils, and eye sockets. (Personally, I love eels—especially when they're smoked.) The act of reading is always a dialogue between reader and writer, and in Hens I have found my ideal interlocutor, which is a great relief to me, because for the committed smoker there's only one thing worse than not being able to smoke, and that's not being able to talk about it.

Will Self, London, 2015

nicotine

I've smoked well over a hundred thousand cigarettes in my life, and each one of those cigarettes meant something to me. I even enjoyed a few of them. I've smoked great, okay and terrible cigarettes; I've smoked dry and moist, aromatic and almost sweet cigarettes. I've smoked hastily, and other times slowly and with pleasure. I've scrounged, stolen and smuggled cigarettes, I've finagled them and I've begged for them. I've thrown away half-full packs only to fish them back out of the rubbish to render them useless once and for all under the tap. I've smoked cold cigarette butts, cigars, cigarillos, bidis, kreteks, spliffs and straw. I've missed flights because of cigarettes and burnt holes in trousers and car seats. I've singed my eyelashes and eyebrows, fallen asleep while smoking and dreamt of cigarettes — of relapses and fires and bitter withdrawal. I've smoked in 110 degree heat and

1

in minus 15 cold, in libraries and seminar rooms, on ships and mountaintops, on the steps of Aztec pyramids, furtively in an old observatory, in basements and barns and beds and swimming pools, on air mattresses and in thin-hulled rubber dinghies, on the prime meridian in Greenwich and the 180th meridian in Fiji. I've smoked because I was full and I've smoked because I was hungry. I've smoked because I was glad and I've smoked because I was depressed. I've smoked out of loneliness and out of friendship, out of fear and out of exuberance. Every cigarette that I've ever smoked served a purpose — they were a signal, medication, a stimulant or a sedative, they were a plaything, an accessory, a fetish object, something to help pass the time, a memory aid, a communication tool or an object of meditation. Sometimes they were all of these things at once. I no longer smoke, but there are still moments when I can think of nothing but cigarettes. This is one of those moments. I really shouldn't be writing this book. It's too much of a risk.

But I won't be deterred. I will write about it all, without mystifying or demonizing it. I regret nothing. Every cigarette I've ever smoked was a good cigarette.

———

There are people I'd really like to smoke a cigarette with: friends I haven't seen for a long time, artists I admire. That this won't come to pass isn't solely down to me and my resolution. Most of them don't smoke anymore. Some of them are already dead. I'd have liked to have smoked with my grandfather, whose huge, calloused hands always made the cigarette look so thin and fragile. He died too soon. I'm convinced that he died because his cigarettes were taken away from him when he was admitted to hospital after a fall, even though he smoked only five to ten a day for sixty years. My grandfather was an extremely restrained man. When, on occasion, he spent the whole morning sitting in his kitchen in Koblenz-Pfaffendorf sorting lentils or peeling potatoes laid out on an old newspaper, or polishing brightly dyed Easter eggs with a piece of bacon rind, the pack of Lux with the matchbook hidden inside lay beside him like a promise.

I often dreamt of smoking in an art museum. I imagined how I would sit on one of those smooth, solid wood benches already warmed by the obliquely angled afternoon sun in front of a quickly painted and austere group portrait by Frans Hals, for instance, and light up a Finas Kyriazi Frères, a filterless oriental cigarette that sadly vanished from the market a few years ago.

I've no doubt that this would be a moment of absolute clarity, perhaps my greatest moment of happiness.

This will never happen. I no longer smoke. But I can write about it. And as I circle the subject of my addiction—a central theme in my life—through writing, I might as well ask myself a few questions: How did I become a smoker? What was it that I needed? Did the countless cigarettes I smoked throughout the course of my life satisfy this need? How did I deal with my addiction alongside the occasional fear of not being able to control it? Was I not afraid of the risks?

There's no need for me to set out my reasons for quitting. Everyone knows the arguments, the social and the medical. Smoking is a compulsive behavior. He who conquers his urges gains his freedom. I've failed often enough to know that I'm right at the beginning. I've decided that this time I'll write my way out of my addiction by telling its story. I'm devoting my undivided attention to a structure that governed nearly my entire life and that at certain times I actually mistook for being life. I took many of my patterns of behavior, automatisms and thought processes for granted; I never even noticed them. It's only now in retrospect that I can engage with them and begin to make sense of them.

Something staggering occurs to me: I've smoked over a hundred thousand cigarettes and with the best of intentions cannot say whether the paper crackles when you light one like in the old cinema ads. I've never noticed, not once.

A service station on the A1 somewhere in Westphalia, Germany, in the mid-nineties. A blue-and-white gas station, the roar of motors and the blare of tires behind dusty West German thorn bushes. I've parked my car and I'm waiting for my brother to take me to Delmenhorst, where our great-aunt lived—a woman whose retirement terms included a century-long, inheritable cigarette allowance.

A Danish big rig rolls to a standstill, the hydraulics hiss. The driver is wearing pleat-fronted trousers and a light-colored plaid shirt. He looks refreshed, as if he just stepped out of a locker room. I sit in front of the shop on a stack of shrink-wrapped firewood, drinking coffee out of a paper cup and looking up into the matt sky. I don't know what to do with the swizzle stick. The Dane comes over, stands next to me and lights up a Gauloises red. He offers me one wordlessly. I point to the gas pumps with the stirrer. Too close, I say in German. Then: *Too close. Boom.* He laughs. A silver-gray Maserati pulls up in front of us. The side window lowers, my brother pushes up his glasses and asks: Been waiting long? I nod to the Dane and walk around the low car. *Boom*, he repeats, grinning and miming an explosion with his hands. Like an exotic flower blossoming in time-lapse, I think, like a New Year's Eve firework. I steady myself, duck my head in, slide into the bucket seat. Stefan looks skeptically at the Dane and then at my paper cup. He doesn't like it when I drink in the car. My father was the same. Stefan pulls away. We don't talk a lot. We smoke, and sometimes Stefan says something like: I don't think she was lonely. Or: Did you know she still went on booze cruises to Heligoland? They are merciful sentences, sentences that I don't have to respond to. They pulsate for a while afterwards before they're drowned out by the sound of the highway, the deep drone of the twelve cylinders. She had made it to eighty-two.

Shortly before we reach Bremen we leave the Autobahn. My brother steers assuredly through the area, he still knows his way around. He's four years older than I am and can remember it more clearly. There's the shopping center, he says, do you remember? And that's the way to the place where we ate kale and pinkel sausage. I try to imagine what I would have seen, what I would have noticed, if I had been a bit older at the time. Once a year on a Saturday afternoon in January, our aunt would pay for the whole family to eat at the best restaurant in Bremen. There was kale and greasy, corned sausages, iced schnapps. I recall wooden benches with padded cushions, thick, rug-like tablecloths, waitresses who would ask disbelievingly if I had finished it all by myself.

We drive past a school. I recognize the red clinker façade, the white railings, and the sports field with its modest stands comprised of six staggered rows of benches. The images are evidently still stored in my brain, somewhere. I remember that children would be running around the playground when we came to visit at the start of the summer. Their holidays began later. They must have seemed very strange to me, as if they lived in another country, in a different time zone. Who were these children behind the railings? Did we speak the same language?

We turn into the residential estate as the wind speeds in the Baltic and North Seas are reeled off on the radio. The estate is composed of white bungalows tucked away behind tall hedgerows and bushes that shimmer with a silvery sheen. A boy on a BMX rides straight at us, pulling off a casual, one-handed swerve at the last moment. The driveway's clear. Stefan drives across the ramshackle flagstones right up to the garage door, which has a dent in it. Aunt Anna sold her car immediately after the accident, she never drove again. She had been wearing the wrong shoes, the clutch had slipped beneath her smooth Jackie Kennedy pumps. The car must have sprung against the garage door in a single jump, like a hoptoad. She'd only had the dent painted over — why hadn't she had it repaired? That wasn't her style.

A middle-aged woman stands in the doorway. She's wearing pink marbled glasses that are far too big for her face, and a fur coat is draped over her arm and pressed to her chest as if she were afraid someone might take it away from her. She seems tense, nervous, who knows how long she's been waiting. We get out of the car. Stefan speaks with her. The woman talks at him insistently in rapid, clipped sentences. I light a cigarette and take a look around the garden. When the house was first built my great-aunt had a swing installed, even though we visited for only one, two weeks a year at that. For the other fifty weeks the swing was a visible sign that something was missing in this house.

The woman hands Stefan a set of keys and a note with her telephone number on it. Have you got thirty marks? my brother asks me. She takes the money that Aunt Anna owed her, gives thanks

with a short nod and walks down the drive. She was
the cleaner, my brother said, sometimes she played
rummy with Aunt Anna. She was the one who
called the ambulance. Fräulein Meyer, Stefan says,
first she called her Fräulein Meyer, then suddenly
her Aunt Anna. I don't believe for a second that
our aunt really left her that coat.

Aunt Anna's house seems to have barely
changed. It has been nigh on twenty years since
I've last been here. A walking frame stands in front
of the bedroom. The mottled, dark red accordion
door that leads to the kitchen is closed. The fan
heater whirrs quietly. I can't find the light switch. I

feel my way around the living room and pull back
a curtain. The room remains dim, the bushes in
front of the terrace haven't been trimmed in a
while. Armchairs—heavy, practically immovable

armchairs with lace covers, armrests wide enough to rest a crystal ashtray on. Armchairs like this always make me think of Deng Xiaoping.

This is where we would often sit and watch *Spiel ohne Grenzen*—the West German *Almost Anything Goes*—and listen to shellac records, which would fall with a clatter from the arm of the record changer, on the sound system housed in a shiny, polished cherrywood cabinet. Aunt Anna knitted colorful acrylic blankets that nobody wanted because they didn't actually warm you up in the winter. The house smelled of chicken and omelette soup, smoke and carpet cleaner. The TV was always on. When the terrace doors were open in the summer and a lighter cooler breeze came in, the Chinese lantern she had brought back from Hong Kong would tinkle above the dining table.

Fresh, balmy peat dug up from the surrounding land was heaped onto the beetroot plants, bushes and the bases of the trees. I knew from my aunt's stories that directly behind the school, immediately beyond the limits of the town, was a mystical place populated by peat diggers and bog mummies. A place, my young brain imagined, teeming with the eternally restless undead, ditch wardens, feral spirits and doppelgängers. Out there beyond the town the peat diggers uncover the skeletons of entire chain gangs, the tiny bodies of unwanted children, the corpses of abortions, bastards and mongoloids. *In the morning the gangs move out to the bog to work. Digging beneath the searing sun, home is what we yearn for.*

On the off-white walls of the living room's vestibule hang mounted and gold-framed photos of work meetings and office parties. In a few of them Fräulein Meyer is alone, and in others as part of a larger group including the chief executive of Brinkmann Inc. Sitting on top of the TV—a Grundig— are several photos of my mother. I tread on the grating of the underfloor heating, listening to its peculiar, resonant rattle and think about all the Lego bricks, marbles and dice I've lost down the duct. Stefan stands in the bedroom in front of the secretaire, he's pulled out drawers, dug out paperwork. With his left hand stuck in his trouser pocket he casually leafs through a small stack of bank statements and correspondence, standing there like he just wants a quick look at the mail after a long day at work. He's looking for a provision order, instructions for the funeral, he explains. Hadn't she already bought a grave plot, picked a coffin and chosen suitable flowers? If we don't find anything, he says, we'll have a cremation. What do you think? Fine with me, I say. Stefan taps off his ash in a pewter plate depicting the statue of Roland of Bremen, as if sealing the deal.

She never owned an address book. She had a sister, our grandmother, with whom she'd been corresponding only via a lawyer for decades, and three school friends who came by once a week to play canasta and milk her generosity. The ladies came by bus from Bremen city center, drank my aunt's good schnapps, ate her homemade cherry cake, played a couple of games and then were gone again. Our aunt went on a round-the-world trip shortly after she retired in 1975 or 1976 with one of them, Elke, who was likewise unmarried. She sent my father the Super 8 films while she was still traveling, and he sent them on to Kodak to be developed. Every one of them came out shaky. My first thought now would be Parkinson's, but back then we just laughed.

I'm sure she paid for Elke to take the world trip too, Stefan says. He must have been having the same train of thought as I was at exactly the same moment. We watched the whole Hong Kong film at the time: the six precious Kodak minutes of the shaking behinds of a pack of German pensioners in Kowloon made a deep impression on me. The way the ladies shuffled across Nathan Road, past the park to the gigantic, filthy Chungking Mansions. I would spend an oppressive summer there a few years later lying on a bunk directly under the sweaty, sloping, greenish ceiling of the sleeping hall packed with Indians, filling a pile of notebooks with my pencil in just my underpants; a good four hundred pages, which never wanted to coalesce and become the great postcolonial novel that I had intended.

I flinch at the buzz of the doorbell. The door's been left open. A man holds out a clipboard and a pen. He asks me to sign and gives me two cartons of cigarettes. He bids me a good afternoon and turns back to his white delivery van standing on the street with the motor running. A mink hangs on the coat rack next to the door. Two fur hats on the rack look warm and lively, like they're only sleeping. Above an old, zinc milk churn offering an abundance of colorful umbrellas hangs a Gloria brand fire extinguisher. I take the cigarettes into the living room.

She never married. Her whole working life, she remained faithful to the Brinkmann Company in Burgdamm, Bremen, a cigarette factory that produced, among others, the market-leading light cigarette Lord Extra. As former president of the works council, Aunt Anna had a considerable pension and a monthly cigarette allowance of a carton of Lord Extra and a carton of Peer Export as wages-in-kind delivered by courier. This allowance wouldn't expire until 2071, a hundred years after the start of her pension, and indeed independent of her own final exhalation, her last expiratory act.

I took such in-kind payments for granted during my childhood. My great-grandfather on my father's side was a driver at the Deinhard sparkling wine cellars in Coblenz and my grandmother commanded a sizable allowance of their product long after his death, which helped her to rise the ranks and become unchallenged queen of the Coblenz black market during the ruinous war years. She exchanged the affectionately named *Bubbes* for butter, coal, potatoes and, of course, cigarettes. The Deinhard cellar was classified as a "critical war supplier" and spent the war years producing wine for the officers' mess. When I told my classmates about my grandmother's dealings, they looked at me blankly, almost as if I'd lost my marbles. My primary school teacher also didn't seem to understand what I meant when I mentioned, in an essay about my excursion into the storage cellar in Pfaffendorf, seeing the allowance of bubbly next to the conserved, unsweetened gooseberries we would eat with cream.

Aunt Anna smoked only occasionally and happily gave most of her monthly ration to our mother, and later to us children. I didn't smoke many filter cigarettes in my youth, only when I didn't have money for tobacco or filterless cigarettes. Sometimes, with a brief flick of my wrist, I would tear the filter out. Though our aunt smoked infrequently, she did so with a peculiar ravenousness, like my grandfather and many other older people I've noticed since. It's as if they'd waited their whole lives for this first drag. Or as if it were their last.

She would stick the cigarette right into the hinge between her index and middle fingers and hold her whole hand in front of her mouth, giving her a shocked expression whenever she smoked. She would inhale deeply and frantically with her eyes wide open, sometimes with a strange, faltering gasp as if she was being suffocated.

It was an open secret in our family that Aunt Anna had always been in love with the chief executive of Brinkmann. The fact that she, as employee representative, was required to maintain an adversarial relationship with the chairman, whom she loved, cast a tragic, almost mythical shadow over her life. Moreover, he was a married man. They were, as I realized early on, the Romeo and Juliet of the German cigarette industry. In the late fifties or early sixties this love must have come close to being fulfilled. Every so often, Aunt Anna would tell us in suggestive words and with shining eyes of a spontaneous journey she had taken to Switzerland, to a lake (I seem to remember it being Lake Lugano), where the chief executive—a stately man with horn-rimmed glasses and a deep tan—maintained a property. When my aunt reached this point in her story she would fall silent, pull a Lord Extra out from its packet with her smooth, stubby fingers, light up and look out into the pewter gray north German autumn sky.

We pick the stronger Peer Export. I fetch a bottle of Güldenhaus Eiswette—a clear, corn schnapps produced in Bremen—from the freezer compartment and pick up two shot glasses and a luminous blue glass ashtray from the sideboard on my way back. It's so heavy you could kill someone with it. Stefan, who's pulled up a chair, grabs his kneecap for support like an old farmer, leans forward, pours to the rim and passes me a glass. I've sunk so deeply into the Deng Xiaoping chair that I can barely hope to ever get out of it again, especially after the Eiswette. I am exhausted.

To Aunt Anna, Stefan says, raising his glass.

To her love, I say.

Outside is the overly high hedge, and the orange-colored awning that we'll have to have replaced before we sell the house. I rip out the filter, flip the cigarette and light up. The hundred-year stipend now belongs to us. Everything that remains from this life now belongs to us.

I once owned a house in the American country-side that hid a gigantic ant colony beneath its gently sloping, prettily laid out front garden. The entire parcel of land was infiltrated. A passerby, throwing only a fleeting look over the place, would have been completely unaware of it. Maybe they would have delighted in seeing the freshly painted, light blue wooden façade, the glorious irises. But the moment I stuck a spade into it, the moment I pulled up just a single patch of weeds or disturbed a mossy slab with my foot, whole armies of combat-ready army ants gazed up at me: powerful, shimmering red specimens evidently waiting only for me. They streamed into the daylight in their thousands, the earth would appear to be in motion, and I'd be seized by vertigo.

I sometimes feel that my addiction lurks under the surface of my life in a similar way. I no longer smoke. You wouldn't look at me and think I had ever smoked. I exercise every day and I'm a member of the German Alpine Association, the Berlin section. I've got my asthma under control and can breathe better than ever before, in fact the volume of my lungs has doubled over the last twenty years. I remember how a biology teacher measured this volume with an apparatus. The students would take turns blowing into a tube that was placed in a beaker filled with water. The displaced water collected in an overflow beaker, showing us our expiratory vital capacity. When the teacher saw my pitiful results he gave me a peeved look. Then he realized I'd given it my all and the annoyance gave way to dismay. I was privately pleased with my result—I'd known for a long time that I had a weak chest. These breathing difficulties would save my skin one day when I was pulled over on a road leaving Düsseldorf and told to blow into a Breathalyzer. No matter how hard I tried, I couldn't blow long and consistently enough for it to beep. The officers got annoyed and let me drive on.

Today I'm a healthy nonsmoker in my best years, apparently, but no matter where I begin my story, no matter where I scratch the surface, I always alight upon cigarettes, on nicotine, on an addiction that had a hold on me most of the time, for most of my life. Whether I actually smoke or not, my personality is a smoker's personality. My story is transfixed by cigarettes, and my body cannot forget what I put it through during those years. The life I led is smoke-screened to such an extent that I have to get very close to even see it. Sometimes it makes my head spin.

I no longer smoke, but today I will acquire my final cigarette. A couple are sitting in a Hollywood swing seat with a gray army-style blanket over their knees in front of a café on a dim yellow street corner in Berlin. They have stopped the swing and are managing to balance only precariously thanks to the grip on the soles of their Pumas. The young woman leans far forward and puts her cigarette out in an ashtray made from punched-out tin that's sitting on an overturned fruit crate. Only then do they let the seat swing again, the man putting his arm around his girlfriend's shoulder. When I see people relaxing like this, I always hear my father's voice in my head: Don't they have something better to do? When my father wanted to grind out the point that the behavior—especially the bad behavior, and especially the laziness—of individual people can affect the whole of society, the term "economic damage" was deployed every time without fail. There are experts in this. For example, imagine you're stuck in a traffic jam heading south. A driver gets out of his car to get a bottle of lime iced tea from the back while the car in front of him has already started moving to make up a few meters. A gap appears. Even though the driver is soon back behind the wheel and has quickly caught up, even though it looks like his actions have had no consequences for either him or the wider community, he has in fact set in motion a delay that extends right to the end of the traffic jam and has possibly affected thousands of drivers, tens of thousands of people, who have lost seconds of their more or less worthwhile lives, easily adding up to a few hours, even a whole working day. A German laborer costs us, let's say, eighty or a hundred deutschmarks an hour, my father would explain, the economic damage is considerable, we've paid dearly for that lime iced tea.

So much for my father's etho-economic lecturing, in which words like "good" and "evil," "injustice" and "morality" had no place. There are in fact departments at big insurance firms and certain university research facilities that calculate how much it costs society if a young woman sits and smokes in a Hollywood swing seat instead of spending time at the gym, reading Charles Dickens, constructing a suspension bridge or peeling cucumbers. Each of these scenarios has its own economic value. If I had journalist blood flowing through my veins, I'd immediately try to get an appointment at one of these departments. But this isn't that kind of book. I'd interview a crazy, eccentric and naturally somewhat unhappy specialist in applied mathematics who would confirm precisely what my father always said — that everything has its price, even if no transaction ever takes place that confirms the value. It just needs to be calculated.

While we're at it, maybe we'd also be able to prove if it's easier for some people to build a suspension bridge or read Charles Dickens while smoking. Peeling cucumbers is a bit different, I think to myself, and approach the couple. I ask the woman for a cigarette. Actually, I think to myself, this economic destruction machine owes me one, after all, she's cost me a great deal. In spite of this my heart's thumping, it's as if I'm doing something forbidden. The languid, mildly distracted gaze of the man meets mine. I'll pay for it, I say, a sentence that's often served me well. It works every time. When I still smoked I would hold out fifty pfennigs or cents, which corresponded to more than a 100 percent markup. It's an offer that the receiver acknowledges but must ultimately reject in order not to come across as an extortioner. Smokers know from their own experience that in certain situations their fellow smokers would pay a lot more for a cigarette, they would give anything for one, but a code of honor prevents them from profiting from the addiction of others.

No worries, she says, and knocks a cigarette out of the pack. I get a Benson & Hedges for nothing and reach over with a smile. On the short way home two things go through my mind: first, that an expression like "no worries" is far more complex than it appears. "No worries" means: actually, you're causing me a great inconvenience, but I'll let you off this debt. I'll decide when it's up, don't forget, I am benevolent and charitable. Second, I wonder if there are rubber gloves in the bucket under my sink.

Back upstairs at the flat I take a clean white piece of paper from my printer, lay it horizontally on the table and position the cigarette on it, centered and exactly parallel to the longer edges. I contemplate the composition, a picture. *Ceci n'est pas une cigarette.* Two dark spots where my fingertips touched the cigarette paper. What I need is a scalpel, but I don't even have a sharp knife. Then the scraper for the ceramic-top oven comes to mind, a razor blade clamped into a black plastic handle. I carefully cut the length of the cigarette from left to right, from the filter to the tip. It feels like something dead to the touch, a mummified worm. Blond tobacco crumbles out. My pores are wide open, I'm sweating a little. I worry that the nicotine will permeate my skin and get into my bloodstream. It's not for nothing that nicotine patches work so well. Rubber gloves, I think again, but that's absurd. Though nothing's really absurd considering the depressing statistics in cases such as mine. The probability that I'll stay on course and lead a smoke-free life is around 8 percent, even without experiments like this. According to scientists, the more attempts at abstinence smokers have behind them, the harder it is for them to stop their consumption of nicotine. See it through, M. says. Get your addiction under control, my therapist says. I don't know how many times I've already tried.

This is the perfect place for a witticism almost universally attributed to Mark Twain that's been cited in every book and every article on the subject without exception and taken up as a motto by countless self-help authors. *Giving up smoking is the easiest thing in the world, I should know, I've done it hundreds of times.* It's curious that so many variations have emerged (A hundred times? A thousand times? Countless times?) and that a reference is nowhere to be found. Not one of these authors wants to divulge which work this all-time favorite Mark Twain quote comes from. I can verify this, I own a whole pile of these self-help books—there was a time when I would receive them very regularly as gifts. Relatives whom I'd seen only two or three times in my life would wink encouragingly as they presented the books to me, the older ones giving me an additional pat on the back of my hand. At some point it stopped, maybe word got around that I couldn't be saved.

As if it would be possible to free oneself from an addiction that has been formed and solidified over years or even decades in ten easy steps, or in fifteen minutes with eight simple rules that anyone can understand. As if it would be enough to stick lists on the refrigerator door or to rub yourself with Ayurvedic oil. An average smoker experiences two hundred to three hundred sharp mini-highs in their brain every day, which results in a measurably higher level of dopamine and the structure of the brain changing permanently and irrevocably. Nicotine is known to be a stronger addictive substance than heroin; children become addicted after only a few cigarettes, some are born as addicts. Should it somehow suffice to do breathing exercises for ten minutes every morning and change your diet? Should one simply adopt the tapping technique of energy psychology and joyfully keep smoking until the problem dissipates? I threw out all these books because their authors are clueless and plagiarize one another unscrupulously, and inaccurately at that. See Mark Twain.

Milan Kundera describes in one of his novels how Goethe and Ernest Hemingway meet in the afterlife and debate the pros and cons of immortality. (Goethe is the enlightened one in this conversation; he's long been immortal.) If Mark Twain were to join this illustrious society, he could tell of the wondrous posthumous proliferation of his quotations. In other words, it appears that sharp wit needs a home, as if these kinds of clever sayings endure only if ascribed to a clever soul. Like viruses, they need a host body to survive. Twain, who was clearly a great connoisseur of human nature capable of expressing his beliefs on all aspects of contemporary life with keen wit and ingenuity, as well as a passionate cigar smoker, is an ideal host for this quote.

Caroline Thomas Harnsberger, a Columbus, Ohio–born violinist and amateur philologist, had already quashed the quote in 1947. More specifically, she rebuked it through disrespect: in her famous volume of quotations *Mark Twain at Your Fingertips*, it isn't even mentioned. Harnsberger, who performed at Carnegie Hall at the age of twenty-two, who later directed an orchestra in Illinois, built up a musical instrument manufacturing business, brought up three children and wrote thirteen books including a reference book for pilots, remains to this day the irrefutable authority on all things Mark Twain. If she didn't find the quote, then Mark Twain didn't write it. Out of respect for Twain the author and as a bow to the revered philologist, I'd rather quote a couple of lines by Van Morrison. He's not particularly known for his biting wit but is always good for getting a sense of life. Plus, he's not plagiarizing anyone.

Well, you search in your bag
Light up a fag
Think it's a drag, but you're so glad
To be alive, honey
Alive, honey.

I don't know whether writing this book will benefit or harm me, whether dissecting the Benson & Hedges will benefit or damage me. It's an experiment. I consciously confront myself with my only recently overcome addiction. I do it because I believe I'm ready. Only those who are caught out by the pull of their addiction, those who are seized without warning, really run the danger of relapsing. That's why M. and I agreed to talk about smoking only if *I* initiate the conversation. She mustn't talk about it, nor may she ask about my withdrawal symptoms. I don't want to be taken by surprise. A comment, a harmless question can strike without warning, like an uppercut. You reel, you topple. For a while I suffered from disturbed sleep; it was truly awful. M. wasn't allowed to mention it. On top of that I'm dysphoric, as my therapist says. Bad tempered. M. serenely and patiently ignored this too. The real withdrawal phase lasted about two months. She kept to our agreement, didn't say anything. Sometimes she gave me a sympathetic look, which was all the encouragement I needed.

The physical symptoms of withdrawal have now passed, and I should begin to mentally adjust to the smoke-free life lying before me. Instead I'm writing this book and thinking of nothing all day but cigarettes. Perhaps this is the moment of inner reflection that must precede my mental conversion. Or it's a self-deception, a continuation of my addiction via other means.

I could write about something else, about endurance sports for example, a related subject that I know just as much about as I do smoking. In both cases it's all about breathing, a fact that never escapes me when I shop at Laufladen Lunge: a running store in Berlin-Wilmersdorf owned, apparently, by the Lunge family. (*Lunge*, it so happens, means "lung" in German.) In my life, smoking and sport belong together; they are, as a linguist would say, in complementary distribution.

I've always either smoked or done intensive endurance sport. Three years ago I completed my first triathlon in a reasonable time. I trained in Austria, in the mountains overlooking Innsbruck. I'd get up early in the morning and ride my racing bike from Tulfes to a clear mountain lake at around

2,400 meters altitude, where I'd swim laps for an hour. Seldom in my life have I felt so relaxed and at peace as I did then. When the cool, smooth fish swept past my legs, I didn't flinch once, I didn't mind at all. Three women would watch me while doing their yoga exercises on a weathered jetty and would occasionally look over and smile. After swimming I would meet my friend Paul for breakfast, read and sleep a little. In the afternoon I would jog for an hour or two across the long-distance walking trail, sometimes alone, sometimes with Paul, whom I met on a forum for endurance sports. My strongest discipline is cycling. A few months after the triathlon

I rode into the side of a delivery van at forty kilometers an hour. I came to as the paramedic was cutting open my tight cycling leggings with a pair of bandage scissors. A second paramedic was pulling glass splinters out of a wound above my right eye with a pair of tweezers. A police officer who was standing behind them asked if he could take down my particulars. He said I wouldn't have survived without a helmet.

Survived what? I asked.

I was pushed down a long corridor and dropped off in front of a radiation-shielded door. I raised my head as well as I could and looked around. The corridor ended with one of the countless double doors battered by wheelie beds and had the word REANIMATION in mirror image scratched into its frosted glass windows. My phone had been in a bag mounted under the saddle of my bike during the accident, and I angled for the plastic bag on the rack under my wheelie bed to get it out and take a photo.

Reanimation isn't the kind of word you want to see from behind, I thought to myself, and called M. I'm in the realm of the dead, I said. I was x-rayed and stitched up, a psychologist asked me for the day of the week and the name of the chancellor, then asked me to complete the sequence 21-19-17...

There are several answers, I replied.

M. finally arrived. She stood beside me and stroked my head while I signed a statement clearing the hospital and its friendly staff of any responsibility should a blood clot form in my brain against

expectations in the days to follow. The ward nurse gave me a pair of operation trousers for the journey home, pressed the plastic bag and my bloody T-shirt into my hands, and discharged me. My right knee was stiff and swollen, my forehead and chin were bandaged. My right hip stung from a twenty-centimeter road burn. M. and my neighbor helped me in the night to get to my apartment on the fifth floor and laid me on the bed. After three days the headache let up. After a further eight days, in great pain, I put on a tracksuit and dragged myself down to the street in my slippers. I bought a pack of Marlboros in the Mai-Thai bar, a seedy establishment in the neighboring building. The girl at the bar watched me, bewildered, while I tore off the cellophane and, trembling, awkwardly yanked at the silver paper. She lit the cigarette for me, a dozen golden bangles jangled on her thin, brown arms. I hadn't smoked in eight years. I staggered outside, grabbed the porch railing to steady myself and cried with happiness. My legs were shaking. I was back. I had seen the gateway to death, from the inside, no less. But I was back. *To be alive, honey. Alive, honey.*

It wasn't my first bike accident in Berlin. A few years previously, I was on my way to a whiskey and tobacco shop in central Berlin rumored to belong to the wife or girlfriend of the poet Durs Grün- bein. I didn't give a damn about that. What I was interested in was the filterless Senior Service that couldn't be bought anywhere else in the city and that were reserved for another patron, presuma- bly a poet. The situation seemed vaguely familiar to me even before I'd got hold of the first pack; the film *Smoke* by Wayne Wang and Paul Auster, in which a similar scenario plays out, had just come out at my favorite arthouse cinema. I had to coax these cigarettes from the friendly lady every time, pack by pack. On the way there, maybe already lost in thought about the delicate task lying before me, I landed on the hood of a red Toyota Land Cruiser. A short time later I was sitting strapped in on a backwards-mounted seat in the ambulance driving in the direction of Charité hospital. The paramedic was sitting next to me and seemed to have nodded off when the ambulance came to an abrupt stop, the partitioning window to the driver's cabin slid open and the driver said: Herbert, I think I've just hit an old lady. The paramedic gave me a weary look, excused himself and calmly climbed out. After a few minutes, with Herbert's support, an old woman clambered inside. Welcome aboard, I called out to her nonchalantly and smirked. But instead of reciprocating my amicable salutation, she was overcome with a bout of hysteria, a violently abusive screaming fit that was still going when we were unloaded at the hospital. Even in the waiting room in the ER she kept hissing at me like I was a metamorphosed Gregor Samsa, poking her crutch at me like she wanted to shoo me into a corner. Only later did I see that my whole face was caked with blood, a four-centimeter-long laceration gaping on my right temple. With my slashed shirt and my hair wet with sweat standing up in all directions, I offered a frightening, zombie-like sight. Even I jumped a little when I discovered myself in the bathroom mirror.

I can still hear the old woman caterwauling in my ears as I turn back to my experiment with the bummed Benson & Hedges. I disassemble the cigarette into its individual parts, I dissect and consider them and ask myself what I'm trying to achieve with this experiment. What are you doing? I hear M. say. She hasn't smoked for a very long time. She also no longer eats meat. She runs twice a week and does yoga. Her skin is radiant, her eyes are light and clear. She smells good. She meditates now and then. But she thinks like a smoker. She was always the one who would remind me to buy cigarettes when we were walking home from dinner. She kept an eye on how many were still in my pack. She always had a lighter on her. She planned smoking breaks when we were out. She always looked for the ashtray the moment we got into a rental car. She knew when I would reach for a cigarette even before I knew myself. Sometimes she would become restless if I hadn't smoked for a while. My addiction was her addiction.

I will dismantle this cigarette and my whole past smoking behavior along with it, I think. By dissecting the cigarette into its individual parts I will expose it, I will make a trusted object into an alien one, perhaps even an alienating one. That is what I resolved to do. But instead of creating as vast an inner distance as possible, instead of considering what crumbles so pathetically before my eyes and at my fingertips with calmness and a clear head, I sense how agitated I am. I feel my heart rate rising like it does on a steep climb. By going into the street and obtaining this cigarette, I have taken a first, decisive step back into addiction. I always found it hard to ask strangers for cigarettes, and this time it took no less effort. My inner restraint has a motivation against it that's clearly stronger, stronger than I want to admit. I knew how great the temptation would be and I did it anyway. The next step, I think, beholding the sliced-open cigarette, is a fresh relapse.

But I continue, making it clear to myself that I no longer smoke. That I'm doing well because of it. I have my pulse back under control. I am a vicarious smoker now, like M., I like it when others smoke. Sometimes I walk around the city and imagine that others are smoking on my behalf. I silently thank the smokers in front of the cafés and office buildings and in smoking areas, imagining that they do it for me, for my inner contentment. I have people smoke for me.

How addicted do you actually have to be to entertain ideas like these? I took the Fagerström Test—used in the field of psychiatry to establish nicotine dependency—many times and at different points in my life, and achieved a perfect score every time.

Of note in this questionnaire is that the time that passes between getting up and the first cigarette is a very good indicator of how strong the

1. How soon after you wake up do you smoke your first cigarette?

    ☐ within 5 minutes [3 pts]
    ☐ 6–30 minutes [2 pts]
    ☐ 31–60 minutes [1 pt]
    ☐ after 60 minutes [0 pts]

2. Do you find it difficult not to smoke in places where smoking is not allowed?

    ☐ yes [1 pt]
    ☐ no [0 pts]

3. Which cigarette would you most hate to give up?

    ☐ the first cigarette of the morning [1 pt]
    ☐ any other [0 pts]

4. How many cigarettes do you smoke on average in a day?

    ☐ up to 10 [0 pts]
    ☐ 11–20 [1 pt]
    ☐ 21–30 [2 pts]
    ☐ more than 30 [3 pts]

5. Do you smoke more during the first hour after waking than during the rest of the day?

    ☐ yes [1 pt]
    ☐ no [0 pts]

6. Do you smoke even when you're sick and have to stay in bed?

    ☐ yes [1 pt]
    ☐ no [0 pts]

addiction is. Someone who smokes forty or more cigarettes a day, but only after brushing their teeth (4 mins), showering (8 mins), getting dressed (5 mins) and having breakfast (20 mins), etc., can achieve a maximum of 8 points according to Fagerström and would be classified as highly, but not wildly, dependent. I have to confess that my perfect score was momentarily jeopardized because I stumbled at question 3. If I were prepared to relinquish the first cigarette of the day (which would knock off a point), the next cigarette would then be my first cigarette and I could enjoy it just as much as the real first one that I so nobly gave up. I would just postpone the second cigarette of the day by ten or fifteen minutes; I would, the way I see it, lose nothing. In the end, in spite of these considerations, I still gave myself a point. I wanted the perfect result, like a friend of mine who drank himself to the edge of delirium the morning of checking himself into an alcohol addiction clinic in order to impress the admitting doctor, and maybe himself. He most likely wanted to establish himself as an expert in withdrawal by making himself the greatest boozer of all time, like a child on a swing who makes themself soar with all their might so as to be able to make an especially impressive jump.

———

I consider the crumbling tobacco of my Benson & Hedges. At one end, the end you light up, it's a little compacted so that it doesn't come apart as easily. This is the so-called reinforced end that prevents the tobacco from crumbling out of the front of the cigarette. (I've read that filterless cigarettes are compacted at both ends, so it doesn't actually matter which end is lit.) The reinforced head is to blame when a lit cigarette goes out if you don't take a drag on it. Once the embers have consumed the reinforced head, the cigarette burns all by itself. I think about all the film

scenes where prostitutes light up a cigarette and lay it in an ashtray after one or two drags. As soon as the cigarette's gone out, the date's over. It still surprises me how long it takes for a left cigarette to burn itself out, and yet it seems like cigarettes used to be more tightly packed than they are today. How long, exactly, is a quickie? *Listen, Mister, it's your time,* the young Jodie Foster says in *Taxi Driver. Fifteen minutes ain't long. When that cigarette burns out your time is up.*

I fetch the electronic scale from the kitchen, lay a piece of paper on it and hold down the button until zero appears on the display. Then I shake the crumbs of tobacco onto it. Still zero, the scale doesn't react. How much tobacco is in a cigarette? According to the manufacturer's website, the CMB-120—a laboratory device used in the production of cigarette prototypes produced by the Burkhart Company in Wedel, Hamburg—can measure a load of 300 to 1,400 milligrams. Most cigarettes, I read, have a tobacco content of less than a gram. My kitchen scale can't register a weight under a gram.

The strands of tobacco are large and small, some very thin, some like fine wood shavings exhibiting a distinctive lighter coloration. I most likely have an American blend composed of around 60 percent light Virginia tobacco along with Burley and oriental tobacco dosed with processed tobacco remnants, the so-called blended leaf sheet. The fact that hundreds of chemicals are then added to this miracle blend, some of which are carcinogenic, provides the most significant topos of the cigarette-deterrent industry and has been publicized without measurable success. Instead of worrying about this or consulting the Ministry for Food, Agriculture and Consumer Protection's published

list, I chose one of the newer, additive-free brands and was always very happy with my selection.

Today, right at this moment actually, is the first time I've taken the trouble to look at the ominous list and realize to my disappointment that there are only 688.34372 milligrams of tobacco in a Peer Export. The ministry clearly has a better set of kitchen scales than I do. It wouldn't surprise me if the second piece of information that jumped out while I perused the list, namely, that an ample amount of ethylene vinyl acetate copolymer is used to seal my long-beloved Muratti cigarettes, remained in my unresolved thoughts for the day and influenced my dreams. What form would they take?

It should be noted that the enormous quantity of additives constantly being shared and circulated quickly shrinks under closer inspection. Most cigarettes are manufactured using only a few of the hundreds of possible additives, amongst which are harmless natural flavorings such as sugar, cocoa and licorice. Even a dangerous-sounding candidate like sorbitol turns out to be a naturally occurring sugar alcohol found in pears, apples and roses.

I put the scales back in the cupboard and turn my attention to the filter that's still partially stuck to the cigarette paper. I carefully pluck apart the cottony material reminiscent of artichoke hair. The fibers of my Benson & Hedges are finer than I remember. I later read that they're 30 to 50 micrometers, a number I can barely fathom. The paper's made up of two parts: the thin, white cigarette paper and the strong filter tip, whose color and texture are apparently supposed to resemble cork, which I suddenly find completely ridiculous. In fact it's totally absurd; cork is obviously prized for being impermeable. I hold the paper against the window and discover a row of tiny holes in the mouthpiece designed to thin out the tobacco smoke and let through the oxygen-rich air. The around 900-degree embers convert the sucked-in oxygen to carbon dioxide and then through smoldering partial combustion (around 500 degrees) to toxic carbon monoxide. The smoker receives enough air through the laser perforations to breathe and smoke simultaneously.

Even if I've already known it for a while, I'm still amazed that there's a shade more tobacco in the cigarette than the length of the mouthpiece suggests. I think it's worth noting in the wider context of our consumer world that most products are packaged and processed in such a way that consumers feel they're getting more for their money, like they've got something for nothing. Which marketing specialist came up with the idea to partially conceal their product? Evidently the amount of tobacco we consume is incidental only when it comes to smoking. It's about the effect, the sense of well-being, the right balance.

I remember the ludicrously thin cigarettes that my friends and I used to roll when we were teenagers because we wanted to make the tobacco pouches we bought in Holland last longer, and because we thought they made us look cool. It wasn't about having more back then. Perhaps this is where the occasionally difficult-to-distinguish difference between a drug and a harmless treat like chips or chocolate can be clarified: while we can't get enough of treats, with drugs one is looking for the right dosage, which only increases gradually in the course of a lifetime.

Of course, there are exceptions to the rule: I once visited Gugging, the so-called House of Artists, a psychiatric hospital near Vienna where some of the famous Art Brut artists live. The poet Ernst Herbeck, who died in 1991, had lived and worked in this house and was the reason for my visit. I already knew that nicotine addiction was a significant indicator for schizophrenia; the smoker rate among schizophrenics is three times higher than in the rest of the population. But I was still astonished when I entered the house and met the first residents on the stairs. It was as if they were having a competition, smoking with a greedy naturalness that I'd never witnessed anywhere else before. They sat on the steps and the windowsills, in the brightly painted corridors. They painted, talked to themselves, drilled wheels of licorice into their ears, rubbed themselves between their toes or rocked in solipsistic displacement, and all of them, without exception, smoked relentlessly. Every drag they took was sucked in as if it were their last, and every one of these patients held their pack in their free hand so tightly and securely with a habitual attentiveness, as if it could go missing at the first distraction. I had no doubt that they would have smoked even more if it was physically possible, especially as many of them were indeed successful artists and didn't know what to do with all their money in the confines of the psychiatric ward.

The visual warning of the cork-brown paper that covers the last millimeters of the strands of tobacco prevents the smoker from burning the paper down to the filter. It's incredible how well it works. I have smoked a cigarette down to the filter two or three times in my life, but only because I was sitting at my desk working.

I scrunch up the paper and throw away the Benson & Hedges Gold dismantled into its component parts, and I give silent thanks to the economic destruction machine who gave it to me. Would she have given it to me if I had told her what I had planned to do with it? I take another look at the consumer ministry's list. I didn't realize how many cigarette brands were available in Germany. I should have studied this a long time ago, if only to equip the heroes in my novels with distinctive tobacco wares, the Black Devil menthol manufactured using potato starch and galactomannan for instance, or a Springwater, pepped up remarkably enough with plum juice concentrate. Other authors, especially those servicing the more popular genres, could profit from this highly evocative list.

He let his Black Devil menthol glide between his fingers before he lit it and looked over at her. She carefully tucked her bright blond hair under her headscarf. Half an hour later, she was lying in an overturned Volkswagen Karmann Ghia at the foot of a gigantic pile of coal, desperately trying to free herself.

All right then, a mother concedes, and grants her third and youngest son—he is five or six years old—permission to stay up to see the New Year in and to go out into the street with the grown-ups shortly after midnight to set off the New Year's fireworks. These are the words that the child's been working towards for months.

This child is me.

Apart from a few evenings with my grandfather—a very quiet man with huge hands that always smelled a little of bread and cigarettes—and my first day of school, which have stayed with similar clarity in my memory, I remember very little else from this time. It must have been New Year's Eve 1970. My brothers had already been allowed to take part in the New Year's festivities in years gone by and their stories had awakened great expectations in me, which would obviously be surpassed.

I was told to take a nap. From nine to half past eleven I lay wide awake in my bed and heard the loud goings-on in the living room. My parents had invited some friends and relatives over to the new redbrick, three-story house situated at the end of a row of houses. Twenty or thirty meters behind the turning bay at the end of the cul-de-sac, behind what appeared to be abandoned garden plots edged by an unkempt hedge, the Bergisch-Gladbach connection to inner-city Cologne swept by every twenty minutes.

When my mother came to wake me, I was already standing in the middle of the room putting on my trousers in the dark. She turned on the light, got me the checked shirt I'd been wearing during the day, went to the wardrobe, smiling, and pulled out the thickest sweater she could find. I stretched my arms up into the air, she pulled the sweater over my head, then stroked the hair from my forehead.

I ran downstairs to the living room. My brothers were already collecting the empty wine bottles set down all around the room, carrying them outside and positioning them in a row at the edge of the pavement. I followed after them. Stefan ran back into the house and soon reappeared with a bag of New Year's rockets that my father had bought a few days before, maybe even before Christmas, at a shop called Kaiser Kaffee. My brother let me take a look in the red-and-white bag, pointed to each individual rocket and told me its special properties.

It's remarkable how clearly I remember this night; it's my first childhood memory that fuses into a story, into a whole. All earlier memories survive only as individual images, individual words or smells, perhaps a look or a touch.

All at once the images begin to move.

I remember nothing of the actual, exact coming in of the New Year, of the good wishes and embraces of the adults, of the clink of champagne glasses. The moment is overlaid with the later repetitions of this sequence that took place over many years following the same pattern, with the same participants. My brothers and I must have run back out into the street immediately afterwards. I see my father stepping out of the house with some of the male guests—they all wore hats, some of them had put up their collars—taking the rockets from my brother and sticking them in the bottles standing ready. There would be, as I found out later on, enough rockets to fill the row of bottles five, maybe six times over. A short while later, when everything stood ready, my mother came outside with the other women. The first rockets were lit on the adjoining plot of land. The sound of laughter and the judder of the last train reached over to us.

My mother wore a short, light-colored musk beaver coat, and her midlength blond hair peeked out from under an electric blue hat she'd knitted herself. My brothers were fighting over the lighter that my father had given them. Both of them wanted to be the first to light a rocket. My mother saw that they wouldn't reach a compromise, also saw that I stood by more or less helplessly. She pulled out her own lighter and a pack of Kim cigarettes from her coat pocket, a white pack with a red, orange and yellow wavy strip under the logo that was supposed to represent a trail of smoke. I knew the brand, of course; my mother smoked ten or fifteen of these cigarettes a day at the time. Later, with mounting depression, her cigarette consumption also rose, and she changed brands.

She pulled out a cigarette, lit up and held it out to me like a treat being offered through the cage bars of a snappy animal. With a slight raise of her chin and without saying a word, she invited me to take the burning cigarette and light a rocket with it.

It wasn't the first time I'd held a cigarette in my hand. The chocolate cigarettes were especially prized by children of my generation because they were vital (and certainly more important than pistols or hats) for acting out scenes from Westerns. In addition, I'd frequently pull out a cigarette from the cup decorated with an iridescent green velour brocade that was always well stocked on the living room table. I'd stick the cigarette between my lips and suck, sort of aping Aunt Anna, who would pay me to play cards with her whenever she was visiting us in Cologne. Although I've never smoked "cold" in adulthood, not even put a cigarette in my mouth on a moving train or exiting a university building in anticipation, I can still remember to this day the herbal-ethereal flavor of the cold tobacco reaching my mouth through the filter. But it was the first time I'd ever held a lit cigarette in my hand.

I accepted it with a reverence that was felt perhaps more truly and deeply than the humble spirit required of me a few years later at my first Communion. I held the cigarette at the very end of the (white) filter, turned around and walked the few steps to the bottles, keeping my eyes fixed on the tiny ember already hooded by white ash. When my father gave a military gesture to signal the launch, I squatted sideways in front of a bottle, half averting my face, and guided the spark with an outstretched arm and squinting eyes towards a fuse. I was so fascinated by the cigarette and its possibilities, I was so amazed by the fact that something could be set alight by such a weak glow, that I didn't even pick the biggest, most beautiful, most colorful rocket. I was shaking. I poked the spark at the strangely stiff fuse only a few centimeters from the neck of the bottle. The ash flaked from the cigarette, and I tried again and again, after my mother encouraged me with a nod, until finally, finally the fuse flashed with a crackle, and my father pulled me away from the bottle by holding me tightly under my arms and lifting me a little into the air.

I forgot to watch the rocket and looked at the cigarette that I still held between my fingers like something dangerous and magical. The spark had all but gone out from poking it at the fuse. You have to take a drag on it, my mother said out of the half darkness, otherwise it'll go out. Of course, I have to take a drag on it. I'd seen the adults—who practically all smoked—do it often enough. My father still smoked at this point too. He worked in his study cut off on the ground floor of the house, and while he worked thick smoke would roll out from under his door and rise into the other levels of the house. When I was three or four, I seem to remember thinking for a while that smoking was his actual job.

My beautiful, taciturn mother stood on the pavement in the cold night with her hands in the sleeves of her fur coat and gave me a half-sad, half-amused look. You have to pull on it, she said again. I pulled. What else could I have done? I took a drag on the cigarette and felt the smoke, which I had imagined to be warmer, fill my mouth, rise into my nose and lie burning on my eyes, which I had to close, while I snorted out the smoke in shock. But before I'd completely released it, I had to breathe in, and so I started coughing on the pavement with burning, running eyes until my mother banged me on the back. My reaction unleashed a wave of merriment among the drunk adults. But on hearing the expelled laughter, I became, in the strictest sense of the word, myself again. Maybe, as I believe today, I became myself for the very first time. My first thought was that the cigarette could have fallen out of my hand during the coughing fit, and I registered with conscious pride that this hadn't happened. Then I noticed a tingly, acidic, unfamiliar feeling in my stomach. I felt dizzy, but it was as if the mild nausea that I'd detected with an almost scientific interest hadn't seized me, but rather a living entity within me; something — and I have to take great care not to speak of it too favorably — that I could claim as part of myself. I believe that in this moment I perceived myself for the first time and that the inversion of perspective, this first stepping out from myself, shook me up and fascinated me at the same time. And I believe that this first feeling of well-being triggered by nicotine — my first head rush — was forevermore entwined with this fascination.

I was confused, stunned, happy, thrilled. Blood pulsed at my temples. There wasn't any time to take in any impressions or glory in the new—perhaps not even yet understood as new—feelings I'd just experienced due to the pressures of brotherly rivalry and my own childish greed for experiences. I quickly pulled myself together. I surveyed the situation, saw that my brothers for their part were loudly and agitatedly begging for cigarettes. *So we can light the rockets.* My mother once again

pulled out her Kims from her pocket, lit two cigarettes at the same time and handed them out to them without a word. I don't know how my brothers fared; I didn't ask them afterwards and haven't to this day. I didn't know for a long time whether my brother Stefan, who was ten years old and who was considered a difficult child, had already smoked or whether this cigarette constituted just as an intense, wholly new experience for him as it had for me. When I sent him a short email asking him to confirm some dates for the book concerning our great-aunt, when she got her pension and when she took her world trip, he wrote without being prompted that his first cigarette was a Lux that our grandfather had given him on a camping trip in the Bienhorn Valley near Coblenz. I had always dreamt—as I already mentioned—of smoking a cigarette with my grandfather, and my brother, I now read, apparently did precisely that. And not just any cigarette: he smoked his first with him, the first, the most important cigarette of his life! Our grandfather Karl, whom we called Chattering Karl due to his taciturnity, gave him this Lux. Presented to him, I think, as if it was the greatest gift that a person can give someone. Presented wordlessly. And it was long before my mother drew her pack of ladies' cigarettes from her musk coat. The most casually made gestures are also always the most beguiling.

I took another drag on my Kim. Now that the initial dizziness had subsided, my awareness took on a new, never before recognized clarity; it was as if a curtain had been pulled back to let in a breeze, a fog bank had been blown away. Before me lay a wide, sharp landscape all the way to the horizon. It was my inner world—my feelings and thoughts—that had taken on distinctive contours in a constellation that I found beautiful. I felt a mental tingling, a delirium, and I remember that my brothers and the adults present, even my parents, appeared strange to me. Triggered by the nicotine penetrating the mucous membranes in my mouth and nose, entering my bloodstream and within a few seconds shooting into my young, malleable brain, I felt and saw, perhaps for the first time, a great experiential context. Life was no longer composed of individual moments, of wishes and disappointments, that pass by indiscriminately and in quick succession; I not only saw images, not only heard single words or sentences, but also experienced an inner world. In this manner, I was offered for the very first time an experience that was narratable. This is precisely why I can remember this night with such completeness, precisely why I can write it in this form.

A rhythm, a cyclical time pattern that accompanies me to this day must have also begun to overlay all my experiences after those first drags. The chemical impulse initiates a phase of raised consciousness that makes way for a period of exhausted contentment. Immediately after the first drags an almost unshakable focus on what's essential, on what's cohesive and relatable, sets in. I often have the impression that I can easily link together mental reactions to my environment that serendipitously arise from one and the same place in the cortical tissue during this phase. This results in associative and synesthetic effects that help me to remember, along with the dreamlike logic that is the basis of my creativity.

Even though I've not smoked for a long time, I still think and work in a constantly repeated rhythm of around half an hour. This consists of an inner impulse, a still physical but now also an endogenous stimulus, and a phase of many-stranded consciousness that levels out in a motion that seems elemental and natural and always at precisely the right time when my body and my spirit can't go on—like a wave smoothly rolling onto a beach. To be more precise, I should really let go of the conjunction, dispel with the old dichotomy and write my body, my spirit, as if they were two words for the same thing, as they are inseparable in moments such as these. I experience the mental processes under the influence of nicotine as something decidedly corporeal—they are powerful or weak, sleek or angular, cold or warm, light or heavy—whereas I experience the body as a mental phenomenon, as something to be understood, learned and remembered.

At the end of this awareness phase, a quick half hour, I feel the incoming (initially only impending) withdrawal phase that I'm not prepared to enter. I defeat the renewed impulse, as I no longer smoke, from my own willpower, from an inner, undoubtedly exhaustible reserve. A smoker would now reach for the next cigarette. Sometimes I just lean back in my chair and turn my attention to the inner processes as set out above. I consider them and wait until what my therapist describes as cravings and what in my Lower Rhenish youth was called *Schmacht*—profound hunger—have passed. It lasts no longer than two minutes.

I took a few more drags on my cigarette that New Year's Eve and lit rockets with increasing assurance. I'd soon learnt to close up the epiglottis in my mouth when pulling in the smoke, protecting me from more coughing fits and the derision of the adults. In the years that followed, we children were given one or two cigarettes every New Year's Eve (depending on how much money my father had spent on fireworks), and it wasn't long before my thrill of anticipation for the cigarettes far outstripped my anticipation for the fireworks.

When I see a firework, I still get the taste of this long, thin Kim on my tongue and remember with great warmth the sad-beautiful eyes of my mother, who handed me cigarettes as if they were something sacrosanct.

I must have already developed an addiction to nicotine, or at least a disposition in that direction, even before this first New Year's Eve. I remember the long car rides on winter holidays when my parents—my father in particular—would chainsmoke. Even thinking about it makes me lightheaded: two smoking parents and three small children driving in a light blue Mercedes 250 S from the eastern suburbs of Cologne to Balderschwang, a journey that in those days required a whole day. The windows were, of course, closed.

Since my father didn't allow eating in his car because of the expensive velour seats, not even a cookie or a drink of water, we would regularly stop. I know that already within the first half hour, in the Siebengebirge hills even, I would routinely feel ill. A couple of times, I can say with some assurance, I had to throw up in some parking lot or other. I'd be in a kind of trance by the time we reached Franconia, an intoxicated stupor I wouldn't wake from until we reached Balderschwang—after thirty or more passively smoked cigarettes. Once the child safety lock was released, I'd push open the door, shuffle out breathing stertorously with an overly acidic stomach, and stagger sleepy and thirsty and strangely excited towards the rented chalet.

It wasn't that long ago that I once again found myself in a glass smoking area in an airport, a kind of suffocation chamber. Repulsed and overjoyed, I came across it while still on the moving walkway, having already pulled out my pack. I stepped

off the conveyor and eyed the box. Eight or ten smokers, all busy with their own rambling thoughts, as if floating inside a cloud, almost as if they were standing on top of a misty mountain peak. The whole box, I feared, could detach itself from the floor and gain height like a hot-air balloon to take us on a long journey into the beyond, perhaps to the gates of hell, perhaps to set us down at an entrance reserved only for smokers. Perhaps it would be the smoke from my cigarette that would create the crucial buoyancy. I lit up even though I would have gotten my kick just by inhaling the thick cubicle air. But with the first puff, I lost myself in thought and forgot about the balloon flight, and I remembered those long trips to Balderschwang, my father's executive saloon, the eternal voice of the radio news announcer and that idiosyncratic tingling in my hands, wet with sweat, caused by the expensive velour.

Scientists replied in the positive a long time ago as to whether secondhand smoke can cause addiction. They also ascertained that people who were exposed to their parents' nicotine intake during childhood, not to mention during the embryonic phase, are without doubt more in danger of becoming addicted than others. They also concluded that people with depression are more inclined to become addicted to nicotine, or people addicted to nicotine are more likely to become depressed. Also known is that the brain's structure changes once it has become accustomed to the nicotine and that these structural changes remain even when the addiction has long been vanquished and normal behavior has been restored. A multitude of rats had to lose their lives for these results. Thousands of experiments appear in publications such

as the *Journal of Personality and Social Psychology* and the *Journal of Addictive Diseases,* most of which have alliterative titles: *Smoking, Stress and Negative Affect: Correlation, Causation, and Content Across Stages of Smoking.* It's amazing what these studies, especially the empirical ones, bring to light: for example, only 61 percent of smokers asked in a survey said that they were addicted to nicotine. The others apparently believe that they smoke only when they want to, and don't grasp that desire is a functional mechanism of addiction. Seventy-eight percent of smokers believe they could stop smoking if they decided to. They're right to a certain extent—but by making this statement they've merely transposed the problem; they're not in the position to make that decision. Why are people unable to fulfill a wish where nothing stands between them and the object of their desire? What does it mean to want something in cases like this?

If one wishes to clarify this scientifically, one must start with Freud, who positioned psychology on a scientific foundation and yet couldn't give up cigars when he was already gravely ill with mouth cancer. (In winter 1898 he encountered the twenty-year-old, practically immortal Mark Twain in Vienna, they moved in the same circles and maybe even bought cigars from the same tobacconists.) Of course there is the possibility of approaching addiction through depth psychology, but I have always had a certain skepticism of the Freudian model because I wasn't sure how to identify evidence to the contrary. What form must the factors take to topple Freud's constructions of thought? Only a refutable theory is a good theory. Besides, from the outset of this pursuit of my addiction, I've had the impression that the explanation for my behavior isn't somewhere deep within my unconscious but barely under the surface; it's actually there for all to see in the structure of my personality. It suffices to narrate what's still clear before my eyes, I don't have to lie on a sofa for that. Most important, I have to change my behavior. What do I do with the situation that I once again find myself in? How do I regard myself? Which mechanism of my thinking, which characteristics do I make use of in certain situations? What can I do to govern my behavior and overcome the automatism of thought and action?

Of course, it doesn't hurt to reread the entertaining Freud and look over the garden fence to see what science, the new cognitive psychology most of all, has to say on the subject. Indeed, I owe some of my reflections to scholars such as Saul Shiffman of the University of Pittsburgh, whose research has focussed on so-called tobacco chippers—those rare, enviable individuals for whom it suffices over years or decades to smoke only one or two cigarettes a day, without ever becoming addicted. Chippers are for addiction researchers what LTS (Long Term Survivors) or Non-Progressors are for HIV researchers: their existence seems to prove that a solution to the problem is within reach. What mechanism is it that separates the lucky few from the masses? Perhaps scientists will one day find the smoker gene or the addiction gene with the help of the chippers; perhaps there's a disposition, a switch that one just needs to flip. But scientists can't deliver all the answers. I'm telling my story because I'm searching for a completely different explanation for why I slipped into addiction. Why did I still choose to poison myself and inflict lasting damage on my brain of my own freewill while knowing of the risks, after being fumigated by my parents, after having to watch utterly sickening anti-smoking films in year seven that ought to have inoculated me against addiction in the style of *A Clockwork Orange*, and even after having to watch a leg amputation on 16-mm film, why did I still choose to smoke for decades? I'm not looking for a gene. I don't want more rats to die. I'm looking for images, stories, the sensory aspect of my addiction. I'm also aware that it won't be enough to talk about it. I have to relearn.

For many people, including me, the disposition to have an evident weakness for all products containing nicotine was effectively determined while still a baby.

The ways into addiction are all very different and this is precisely why it is necessary to tell them. Besides the normal ascent routes (as mountain climbers like to call them) I've already covered, there are some interesting alternative ones. M., who grew up in a small, backward village in Dalmatia, told me that when she hurt herself as a child, she was treated with brandy and tobacco. The cut would be washed out with home-distilled plum schnapps and plugged up with a quantity of hand-cut tobacco before being bandaged. The tobacco would dissolve into the wound over the course of days and weeks until it had melted into her small body, or so the girl must have thought, or would even perhaps still be wet under her skin after the bandage had been taken away. M. would go on to smoke up to sixty cigarettes a day; she spent nearly all the money she made doing her bookseller apprenticeship on cigarettes.

As I'd suffered from so-called chronic or spasmodic bronchitis since earliest childhood—a diagnosis that wasn't really a diagnosis and was consequently never confirmed—I was sent for three weeks to a health spa somewhere in southern Germany at the beginning of my second school year, one or two years after that New Year's Eve. The diagnosis simply described the symptom of a recurring impulsive or convulsive mucus congestion and inflammation of the bronchial tubes. Up to that point I'd always been tucked up in bed with a few consoling words whenever I had one of these attacks. My breath was heavy and rattling, I actually thought I would suffocate, and for an hour coughed my mucous heart out. When I'd finally overcome the acute attack, completely lifeless and with a thin but audible whistle in my lungs, I would lie on my back, as I intuitively knew that any movement, any agitation, would make an additional breath of oxygen necessary, which I just couldn't muster.

I can barely remember this first stay at the spa. It felt like a very long time, and I was glad when my parents finally drove down the driveway, crunching the gravel in front of the building to bring me back home, even if they did suddenly feel very unfamiliar to me. The following summer—and this is where my memory is far sharper—my Aunt Anna took me with her to the Frisian island of Borkum. A doctor had told my parents that the higher ozone content in the northern sea air would be good for me as the irritation would encourage expectoration, and though he hadn't prescribed this trip, he recommended it urgently.

Most of the doctors I've had dealings with in my life should have their licenses revoked. Incidentally, having lived in the United States for many years, I have learned to really appreciate the American liability system, whereby medical malpractice and incorrect diagnoses can result in absurdly high (from a European perspective) penalties and compensation payouts. If you have only ever dealt with European doctors, you cannot possibly imagine how reassuring this threat of legal action is for patients. I still clearly remember an orthopedist in Cologne who treated my mother (who was effectively under his spell) telling me one day when I was about twelve years old that holes had developed in the cartilage in my knees. From that day on, he said, I shouldn't ski or ride a bicycle and must avoid using stairs, especially going down, at all costs. I should also expect to have stiff knees by the time I was thirty. He then prescribed me ten mud packs and sent me home for what I thought would be a life of immobility. I'm now forty-four years old and have recently, as I've mentioned, completed a triathlon in a reasonable time, and take eight- to ten-hour mountain walks whenever it suits me. I can't imagine how my life would have turned out if I'd followed this apparently well-regarded doctor's instructions. Maybe a light would have switched on thirty years later and I would have understood that at the time I had had a choice between a mobile and an immobile life, a choice my mother's ortho-pedist made without thinking for two minutes about the enormous consequences that his instruc-tions would have had on my life, not to mention the national economy. I would quite possibly have stiff knees today.

The good, ozonic North Sea air was what brought me to Borkum. The healthy, bracing climate was — apart from my father's newly discovered passion for sailing — also the reason why my parents bought the mansard-roofed house in Flanders. I clearly remember my mother standing before me in the small kitchen in Cologne trying to explain the correlation to me, her eight-year-old son, as well as she could. She stood leaning against the sink unit with her legs crossed at the ankles, looking very pensive. I focused on the acrylic flowers glued to the tiles behind her while she blew smoke over my head, and after she had guided the irreversibility of my condition right before my eyes—which could, according to her, only be calmed but never cured—her gaze roved out the window. Back then I already knew that eight kilometers away in a northwesterly direction, yellowish, acrid smoke was being emitted from the smokestack of the Bayer plant in Leverkusen, one of the biggest chemical facilities in Europe.

It was only years later, when tennis balls were no longer white but neon green, when *Empfangsanlagen* in airports were no longer called *Empfangsanlagen*—receiving stations—but *terminals,* when the first forest damage reports landed in the first paper-recycling bins and a huge hole suddenly opened above the Antarctic, back then, when the first progressive citizens disposed of their CFC-contaminated fridges and most of the Green politicians of the new movement stopped knitting in parliament and set aside their needles in embarrassment, that the ozone—and along with it the word "ozone"—experienced a radical revaluation. It was at this time that citizens' relationship with their ozone first flailed. Suddenly, from one day to the next, the harmless irritant gas became the arch enemy and the ominous term for the poison was given the suffix "-alarm" to form a composite that evoked the British bomber groups of World War II. The *Ozonalarm* was the logical successor of the *Fliegeralarm*—the air-raid warning. Once again there was an invisible danger delivered from above, from which there was no effective shelter.

I spent the days on Borkum in a seawater wave pool and wasn't sick once. Aunt Anna took extended walks and always brought me back something: sweets, shells. I don't remember much else from this holiday. Later, much later, I found out that my chronic or spasmodic bronchitis was (and is) asthma provoked by allergens. As house dust and dust mites (who love to romp in duvets, pillows and old mattresses) belonged among the provokers, I shouldn't have been tucked up in bed during my shortness of breath or choking fits under any circumstances. It would have been far better to have sent me out to play in the garden for half an hour. I remember a big, beige-colored woolen carpet covered in a dark brown gridded pattern in my childhood bedroom that, without straining my power of imagination, offered itself up as an extensive, very American street grid for my Matchbox cars. I spent entire afternoons lying on my stomach, pushing cars along, sniffling with itchy eyes on this carpet warmed by the sun. I still have the somewhat musty, tickly scent of the unwashed natural fibers in my nose today.

The relief I experienced on Borkum had less to do with the bracing Frisian climate than with the guaranteed dust- and mite-free wave pool and the freshly renovated and newly furnished hotel room that Aunt Anna paid for with her lavish Brinkmann pension.

Three in the afternoon, M.'s out. I'm standing two steps in front of my cleared desk, the sun falls slantwise through the large window. I breathe in. I breathe out. I seek out a place just under my nose where the air streams past. I focus my attention on my breath as it passes this spot, every single molecule. My mind is like a gatekeeper making sure no one sneaks in unnoticed. I observe my air as if there were really such a thing as my air. We tend to believe that every noun refers to something tangible, to a creature, a thing, at least a condition. But words can deceive us, they can lead us to believe that a particular thing exists. What is it supposed to be—my breath? Does it constitute my respiration, the functional structure, the positive and negative pressure generated by my diaphragm? Or is it perhaps the forty-odd-year history of my breathing, which is, despite my predisposition, quite a boring

74

story with countless repetitions? Does it indicate the three to five hundred thousand cubic meters of air that I have breathed and—if I reach average age—am yet to breathe? Or only a single intake of air in this moment, a huff verified with a pocket mirror—my life's breath? Like so many words, the word "breath" also disintegrates as soon as it undergoes a precise inspection, practically nothing remains of it. The only thing that can be proven to exist are my lungs, whose cells are continually being replaced. And the air that I breathe in and breathe back out in a new composition. And my will to live. Even my lungs are no longer the same organs that I exposed to one filterless Pall Mall after the other when I was sixteen. Not a single cell, nothing whatsoever remembers those times. The same goes for the cilia in my bronchi, responsible for the removal of tar mucus, which was thankfully replaced long ago. Breath, breathing, breathed air: I've struggled with it for as long as I can remember. I could never get enough of it. Because I wanted to live. When I ran or hiked or swam, I was always out of breath before my muscle power was exhausted.

I slowly breathe in, I slowly breathe out. I'm now completely relaxed and begin my exercise. I imagine that a grass-green pack of Salem Nº 6 is lying on my desk.

I stand there, motionless, I don't give in to the impulse that ambushes me in this moment. I let the time that I've allowed myself to pass. There's a beeping from down below, a truck is reversing in the

industrial yard, the drink delivery for the Mai-Thai bar. I breathe in. I breathe out. I focus on the place under my nose. My arms hang slack at my sides. I don't reach out. Why don't I give in to my urge? It's more than a desire, it's greed. I tell myself it's a craving. Only it's different from the craving my therapist talks about, it's not over after two minutes. I've chosen this kind of experiment because I'd like to maintain this tension over a longer period of time. I'm interested in what comes after, I want to know what comes when the two minutes are up. What lies beneath? I set out into the terra incognita of addiction.

I slowly breathe in, I slowly breathe out. Do I reach out for the cigarettes or do I leave them there? I could take the two steps, rip open the pack, take a cigarette and light up. In less than a minute I could take the first drag, and the whole nightmare would be over. But do I even have a choice? Ultimately I have placed myself in front of the desk because I have decided against the cigarettes from the outset. And yet the eventuality that I will reach out is actually accounted for within the confines of my experiment. It must be included, otherwise my restraint counts for nothing.

I hesitate, I waver, I persevere. I don't say yes or no. Time stands still. Nothing moves. I can't move because I don't have an answer to the question I'm asking myself. I'm missing an inner instruction. I have the feeling I could do myself damage, no matter my conduct, as if I could break or rupture something within myself, maybe some fibers in my heart. (One breaks the will of a person, one breaks his resistance. One pulls oneself free when one is trapped.) Am I really trapped? Or can I not cope with my freedom? There's no actual reason to do one or the other. There are the cigarettes, and here is my desire. I imagine that the desire doesn't belong to me, but to the object of my consideration, my desired object. For a moment it seems that it's a property of the object that I desire. My will no longer belongs to me. I shelve everything that could lead to a decision. I am completely empty.

It wouldn't hurt anyone if I took a cigarette. I don't need it, I just want it. But I deny myself it—because I can. When it's particularly difficult to abstain, I tell myself: I can take it, but not now. I can take it in ten minutes if I feel the same as I do now. I always conduct this kind of conversation with myself in English, and I imagine that it's Milton H. Erickson, the founder of modern hypnotherapy who died in 1980, who is speaking to me in his inimitable fatherly and serene way. If you believe, I hear Milton's voice say, that this object means something to you, if that really is the case, then you can have it now or in a short while, you do have the option to take it, no one's stopping you, you can do it at any time. If you leave the object for a little while, you can also have it later. You can see that it's lying ready for you. You can sense that you can take it, it is really there. The effort is minimal, you can take it anytime, soon, it costs you practically no effort. If you concentrate on the object, you can perhaps also sense that you can leave it there. It's not really that complicated, and you can decide soon. No matter whether you take it or not, there's very little you need to do. You actually have it already, if you want it, you have it right

before your eyes. And when you don't want it, you don't need to do much since it's lying in front of you. It's still there, like it was to begin with. Look within yourself and try to work out whether you've decided one way or another, try to find out what's preferable or more important, the object lying there as it is, or the wish to take it from its place.

Erickson's words, or rather what I imagine them to be, open up intermediate spaces; they briefly make the floor tremble beneath my feet. Everything seems to swim within them. Erickson is the person I would have liked to have met if any such wish had ever been offered to me. If I told M. about these conversations with myself, she would call me insane, I think. Maybe she'd even leave me—but I know that's not true. It's only a thought reflex, a worry about nothing, which has more to do with myself, the way I perceive myself, than with M. She understands my explorations. She knows what path I'm taking.

I don't step closer to the table. I don't lean forward, I don't reach for the cigarettes. I look at them. Rather than regarding them, I regard myself in this situation. What I have in my sights is my relation to the invented pack of Salem, I consider the unbridgeable distance, the power relation between me and the object. I feel an impact, an almost physical pull, as if the cigarettes are drawing me towards them. The object wants to claim my full attention, nothing else should interest me. I call into memory that I have freely suspended this power. I must not give in. I have called up the spirits, but I know the incantation that will dispel them.

What should I do now? There is nothing left but to either remain in this charged relationship or to break off the attempt. At no point have I succeeded in ignoring the object or the power it emits. On exhaling I feel, presumably from the exertion, a faint resistance, a brink that I didn't want to exceed. From that point onwards I breathe more shallowly than before, change the course of the air earlier than I would have liked. It's difficult to manage this discrepancy in my breathing. *Relax, and let my voice lead you.* Luckily I've done exercises to control my breathing since earliest childhood. I know I have to start with my pulse. Once I've slowed my pulse rate, I'll be able to get my breathing under control.

I have allowed the full effect of this power. I haven't hidden from it. For a moment I toyed with the idea of comparing this impasse between me and the object of desire with a game of tug-of-war where nothing seems to happen. Both teams hold their positions, neither side gives up even a centimeter. The nevertheless enormous strength can be seen in the contorted faces of the opponents, the heels of their shoes pressed into the mud. But this comparison is flawed. I'm not, I now notice, exerting myself. Not that much. And I also know that right from the start I haven't had to exert myself, not in the sense that my power threatened to diminish at any point. The power, this other power, which came completely from within and is apparently inexhaustible, worked all by itself. That I reacted physically, that my breathing went a little haywire, was perhaps only the result of a habitual way of thinking, in accordance with a pattern of behavior that I activated. I saw myself as part of a field of tension and believed that the pulling and tugging could bring me to the edge of exhaustion.

That's enough. I breathe in, I breathe out. I count to ten. M. will be back soon. I turn and leave the room as if nothing had happened. I actually feel refreshed. I didn't reach for the cigarettes, that's an objective fact. The fact lingers. It is valid even though the thought game from which it arose has concluded. The memory of the object has not expired, but it seems as if the tension that it generated never existed. I didn't forgo anything, I didn't deny and I didn't compromise. I listened to myself and made a decision.

During the years of the economic miracle, my father, a technical expert, built up a modest but profitable business that exclusively examined fire and explosion damage in industry and middle-sized businesses. The smaller of these incidents, mostly office and workshop fires, were predominantly caused by cigarette butts, but also by advent candles, Christmas trees and fireworks, which gave the business a seasonal character. At least most of the time. The elephant in the room was, of course, arson.

He smoked up to two packs of Ernte 23 a day. In each of these hinged jumbo packs were forty cigarettes lying beneath silver paper evocative of a freshly ironed bedspread. This meant that my father smoked constantly whenever he was in his home office, which was often, or when he drove to inspections. Shortly after I'd taken my first drag that New Year's Eve when I was five or six, my father

83

went from smoking one day to stopping the next. He didn't, as far as I know, announce this resolution, though he later enjoyed narrating what had happened immediately prior to the decision: he was standing at his desk and had lit up a cigarette while on the phone even though the previous one was still burning in the ashtray, a tin dish with three soldered rivets that looked like finger nails. He apologized and hung up. He understood that he no longer had his cigarette consumption in hand, control had slipped away from him. That was it. That was the whole story. And every time he told the story, he pointed out with undisguised pride how without preparation, without a word of advice, without aids and strategies, he had quit smoking. He had followed none of the typical methods recommended in self-help books. The short story, which soon became formulaic from all the retellings, was laid out solely as proof of the enormous willpower of its heroic storyteller. It's true, he seemed to say, that most people don't manage it because it's actually a perilous addiction. But I did it. It's damn hard, but if you have a strong will like mine, it's in fact no problem at all. If you can't do it with the power of your own will, you are simply a weak person.

One day while we were on a skiing holiday, my father's office caught fire. This lead to countless jokes and ironically twisted remarks within his business circles, which my father would recount over dinner. The following year he sent 120 Gloria brand fire extinguishers as Christmas gifts. The boxes were already piled up in the corridor in

November and in the staff engineer's office next to my father's. All I knew about the engineer was that he'd fled the GDR and that he also used to smoke. His flight over the inner-German border and his abandonment of cigarettes years ago were always connected in my mind; for a while I even held them to be two parts of one, courageous act of will. Every now and again I actually imagined the young engineer with the brown suit and brown briefcase (that's the only way I knew him) jumping over a low fence and flinging the burning cigarette midjump before landing on our side. He was now

a free man. My father didn't know anything about my daydreams; however, he hinted at his own correlation: he considered him, not least because of his GDR past, to be tight with money. This, he suspected, was the only reason he managed to quit smoking. It was made clear to us children that there ultimately had to be some reason or other. We quickly learned that there was only one person who had the ability to succeed without any reason or help, practically without a cause.

Since my father had to buy a set quantity of the Gloria fire extinguishers to get a discount, there were more than a few left over after the Christmas holidays, which had to be distributed among every room in the house. Even in my tiny bedroom, a bright red fire extinguisher hung on a bracket next to the door. The safety pin exercised a power over me that I could resist only with a great deal of effort. Almost every evening before the light was switched off, I considered the miraculous instrument and felt the urge to release the safety pin, a titillation, a tense and blissful feeling that I never once gave in to. I was a good boy.

The secretary, the only other person apart from my father and the engineer to work at the inspectors' office on the ground floor, was to blame for the fire. She had forgotten to put out the candles on her advent wreath before driving home. Through her carelessness she'd initiated a smoldering fire, my father explained, always one to keep up linguistic and terminological accuracy, which he considered the sole domain of German engineering. Hydrogen chloride, a caustic, acidic vapor, which I now know can irritate the mucous membranes and cause an inflammation of the bronchi and lungs, had formed when the desk's PVC lamination had burned up. I learned what a smoldering fire was in the earliest years of my youth. From Aunt Anna living in Delmenhorst in Bremen, I actually had an exact image of what a peat fire was, how it smelled and how it can spread beneath the earth without being noticed. I also knew that a fire, even if completely put out, can reignite spontaneously, as there could always be residual embers. I have never in my whole life put a cigarette out near the edge of a garbage bin, for example, and I have always waited a few minutes before emptying out an ashtray.

There are no longer any coal ovens in the nicer suburbs of Cologne, so I naturally assumed that the inscription NO HOT ASHES that first appeared as orange stickers on trash bins and that was later embossed directly onto their lids referred to cigarette ash. I knew that even if ashes had no visible spark within them, they could still conceal danger. It wasn't until my parents had an open fireplace built in our living room and my father gave us a solemn safety briefing right before the equally solemn first fire, and after we were allowed to help clean the fireplace the morning after the fire had completely gone out behind the steel net guard, that the penny dropped and I understood what the inscription meant. Incidentally, I discovered these bins with their stamped lid in German—KEINE HEISSE ASCHE EINFÜLLEN—while taking a walk through Berkeley, California, in 1990. The city of Berkeley, known for its unorthodox administration, had apparently inherited a job lot from Germany.

When I was about eight years old, my parents bought the summer house in Flanders, a few kilometers from the Western Scheldt and the open sea. This small, typical Dutch mansard house was heated by a compact black oven that stood in the living room and would be adimpleated with briquettes. (The German correlate of "adimpleate" is a technical term used in coking plants, blast furnaces and waste-burning facilities, which my father uses to this day when talking about his espresso machine. He has other verbs in his vocabulary that can be flexibly employed in heavy industry and high-tech pensioner households.) The egg coals glowed white behind a vertically arranged row of elongated glass elements, a kind of transparent picket fence. The narrow panes were so hot that when I was a bit older and home alone or when friends came to visit I'd light cigarettes simply by making contact with the glass. There was so much ember after this first touch that I never had to rush to bring the cigarette to my mouth to take the redemptive first drag. Anyone who's ever tried to light a cigarette on an electric stove-top knows what I'm talking about. The stove gets so hot you can't put your face near it. You light the cigarette without having to take a drag. Most of the time it's no more than a spark, a tiny glow that lasts for a second on the edge of the paper that gets ignited to such a point through multiple short, hectic drags that it virtually starts feeding itself. Sometimes—surprisingly seldom, actually—the spark spreads itself across one side of the cigarette instead of taking hold of the whole of the tip. Experienced smokers know that they must calmly keep smoking, without forcing it to do anything, until the problem vanishes into thin air, so to speak.

On our hurried return from the winter holiday, we established that soot mixed with acid, caused by the smoldering fire in the office, had risen up the staircase into the other floors of the house. The whole house had to be renovated. After that it would always smell of paint, very rarely of cooking—my mother prepared, if she cooked at all, almost exclusively frozen food—and now and again my mother's light cigarettes. The heavy cigarette smoke that had risen from below and stained the walls yellow, which I connected to the enormous industry and drive summoned up by my father time and time again, was displaced for good. If I remember correctly, my mother smoked less in this period, maybe only a couple of cigarettes a day. She must have been doing well at the time, shortly before her best friend, the mother of my playmate Elisabeth, took her own life. (We children were provided with the obviously improvised, somehow child-appropriate explanation that she had fallen off her bicycle.) Throughout her life, before she succumbed to her own melancholy, the psychic condition of my mother could be read on the one hand from her cigarette consumption and on the other hand through her relationship to literature. In the depressive phases, she smoked a lot and read a lot, exclusively biographies and low-brow romances. When she was doing okay she smoked less and read less but with more concentration. She preferred the classics and the modern classics. She read Robert Musil and Thomas Mann, she read Stefan Zweig, Arthur Schnitzler and Joseph Roth, and she warned me emphatically against Franz Kafka, considering his brilliance to be liable to corrupt the young—questionable for a woman who gave her youngest son the name Gregor and never provided a satisfactory explanation for this choice. I wasn't yet ten years old and I had to promise her not to read *The Metamorphosis, In the Penal Colony* and *The Hunger Artist* before my eighteenth birthday, and I kept this promise, even though she died before I came of age.

The most insignificant city in the United States is Columbus, Ohio. It has such a bad reputation among the few people who have heard of it that the defiantly defeatist inhabitants have come up with the motto *It's not that bad.* Columbus primarily exists for the gigantic university where I've held my syntax seminars for years, and is famous for its truly shattering mediocrity. This is where fast-food chains try out their products, this is where the figures add up: the proportion of people of color, rich people, fishermen, vegetarians, coffee drinkers and Buddhists corresponds exactly with the demographic of the American population. Every twelfth inhabitant has diabetes.

The amateur pilot and Mark Twain researcher Caroline Thomas Harnsberger lived in Columbus. She died in the First Community Village retirement home on Riverside Drive in 1991. On an undated postcard reprinted in the local paper, *Grandview This Week,* you can see her photo in an oval cutout.

I have an appointment with Jay Perry, MS. I don't know what MS stands for. He was recommended

to me as a psychologist and hypnotist, as well as — and this is what my trust is founded on — being a member of a regional Milton H. Erickson Society that presides over the legacy of its illustrious founder.

I took great pains not to prepare too well. Through my work I have access to the largest library association in the world and tend to read everything on a subject before I take my first steps into a new area, no different from M., who already knew the Bohemian grandmaster Wilhelm Steinitz and his marvelous opening moves before she sat down in front of a chessboard for the first time (and lost). I rattled my Feldenkrais therapist by telling him about my extensive reading in our first meeting and even freely quoted a couple of lines from Feldenkrais's early study *The Case of Nora: Body Awareness as Healing Therapy*. I won't make the same mistake again, I think to myself, and mount my new racing bike supplied by a German insurance company. I don't mention that I know a lot about hypnosis, autosuggestion and meditation, nor that I've read practically everything I could find on the subject without raising suspicions of being an occultist. I won't say anything about my extended attempts at hypnotizing myself, and I certainly won't say anything about Milton's voice keeping me company some afternoons. I will sit down, close my eyes and keep my mouth shut.

I've actually put off having hypnosis for too long; I almost feel that I'm keeping an obligatory appointment. What's making my heart beat faster isn't the prospect of a healing trance but the new racing bike rolling smoothly and noiselessly northwards along the Olentangy River cycle route. I should have made this appointment sooner, I think, right after I smoked my last cigarette with M. and a Munich friend of ours. Eight months have passed, and on the telephone I was already finding it hard to put it into words. After he'd asked me a few questions, Jay Perry seemed surprised that it was now, after the worst phase was clearly far behind me, that I wanted an appointment for tobacco cessation.

To embed it on a deeper level, I said, to anchor it, you never know.

Later, as we sat in his treatment room, I told him about my bike accident and the first cigarette that the Thai girl had lit for me. I told him how greatly I feared relapsing if something like that happened again. I even went a step farther, a step that only a really good, an excellent psychologist (or former addict) would be able to take with me. In secret, I told him, I sometimes wish that I would have another accident. I wish that something comparably dreadful would throw me off track. Because if something bad, something really awful happened, I could start smoking again. No one, least of all myself, could criticize me, no one would condemn me for it.

Jay Perry had instructed me to bring an audiocassette, an assignment that completely overwhelmed me. In cases like this I always go to Emma, the secretary at the institute where I work. She opened a humble-looking door, more of a hatch, that I'd never noticed before, even though I've worked there for fifteen years and go in and out of the secretary's office daily. She indicated for me to wait, slipped inside and returned a little later with a sixty-minute TDK. We've still got it all, she said. If you ever need tracing paper, dictation tapes or a colored ribbon for your typewriter...Why do you need a cassette anyway?

She grew up in the Taunus region near Frankfurt and also spent a couple of years in Kyoto. I don't know what brought her to Columbus, which she found in her stoic way not only bearable, but actually quite wonderful. I mumbled an answer.

Hypnosis! Emma repeated so loudly that the whole institute must have heard it, isn't that dangerous?

I'd wondered the same thing, and a few scenes from literature came to mind that suggested just that, among them a wonderful chapter from Leonard Cohen's novel *The Favorite Game*, where a boy tries out his magical powers on a number of pets before testing them on his beautiful babysitter. The reader realizes long before the young protagonists that Heather, the ukulele-playing au pair from Alberta, is only faking her trance. It's awkward for both parties when she finds her panties behind the sofa after the hypnosis has ended.

I put the cassette in my bag and ride off. The town extends out towards the north like lukewarm zabaglione—it smells like it too—but after a few miles I reach Worthington, a pretty, clean suburb where the upper middle classes have resettled so they can offer their children the best schools and germ-free swimming pools. *It's not that bad.* There's a Belgian-run French bakery here and a public park with several well-maintained tennis courts. You can guarantee that no one smokes in Worthington anymore. You'll get a sharp look here for just reaching into your bag to take out a note with the address of a hypnotist on it. There are also no fumotopes here, the small, conspiratorial gatherings out in front of bars and office buildings that I've always considered with a mixture of envy and pity. There are only ice-cream-licking children and hybrid cars and I'D RATHER BE GOLFING bumper stickers.

A rather Californian arrangement, actually, Shangri-La, which is why I'm not surprised when I cross a joyfully splashing brook and once more find myself suddenly in a place seemingly in its own world. Rush Creek Village is the name of the settlement made up of twenty or thirty prairie-style houses from the 1950s, the original expression of modernist America. I take another look at my note. The hypnotist lives in the very first house. I slip the racing bike past a white off-road truck into the driveway. I suddenly see the hypnosis in a completely new light. I've booked myself an hour in one of these houses. If the hypnosis doesn't work, I reassure myself, I can at least take a look around the house in peace, it will be fine either way. I won't doze off, I won't close my eyes, I think as I lock up my bike.

I'm a little early. A couple emerges from the house, the psychologist wishes them goodbye at the door. Come in, says Perry, touching my upper arm and drawing me into the house. Three steps lead down to the sunken living space. The house is built on a slope, and the eye is drawn to a thickly forested hollow, the brook flashes through the trees in the distance. He leads me down another flight of stairs. At the end of a tight corridor we step into his study, which has a shabby, worn charm like the rest of the decor. You can't miss that he lives alone

and has for many years. This is the house of someone who'd decorated precisely to his own tastes, everything seemed to fit with him, with his work, his entire being. A corrective hand is nowhere to be seen, no one says to him in moments of doubt that something doesn't match.

Perry falls into an armchair. There's nowhere for him to stretch his legs. He folds his hands and lays them over his crotch. He definitely looks a bit like a rodent, I think, but there's something else. It's a while before I realize that he reminds me of Art Spiegelman's mice, their tapered, almost mouthless faces. First he tells me that he's Catholic and that he meditates, and that during meditation he prays, or more precisely he pray-meditates, a disclosure that I hadn't solicited and that I acknowledge with a skeptical look. I can't imagine how that's supposed to work. Even if I knew how to pray, even if my God had a voice like Milton H. Erickson, I find it hard to understand how mindful meditation fuses together with fervent, imploring entreaties or even simply with friendly conversations. How can I, while I attempt to quiet all inner voices, speak with my God, the father, the all-powerful? How can I practice pure contemplation when I'm eavesdropping on the voice of a capricious God, when I'm despairingly attempting to comprehend the words being directed at me? What do I have to do to be worthy of his love? Why doesn't he speak to me? How do I evade his wrath? Whom could I pray for, what do I have to confess, where have I failed? Is awe not just a prolonged state of fear?

How can I contemplate in this condition, how can I breathe freely?

Perry's not a wise man, I think. That's a pity. I've always wanted to meet a truly wise man. I got my hopes up when I saw the house. My wish has not been granted up to now. It's possible that it's up to me, I'm probably not yet ready for such an encounter. The wisest man I've ever met is Charles J. Fillmore, a linguist born in 1929. He can plausibly and in a falsifiable way explain why it makes sense to ask what your shoes are doing on my bed, even though they're of course not doing anything. But Fillmore lives in California. Notwithstanding Czesław Miłosz, John Searle and Herbert Marcuse, California and wisdom are difficult for me to reconcile. It's also not a question of age. I would guess that Perry's in his midfifties, and I can sense that he still won't be a wise man when he's eighty. When he left university at the end of the 1970s and opened his practice, every household at least had a cassette recorder. Back then people still knew what a TDK is.

The bulky, dark blue armchair that Perry directs me to is clearly left over from that time. I wonder how many smokers have sat here before me. The armrests are worn; gray, rubbery netting is surfacing from under the blue pleather. Perry excuses himself, he needs to go to the bathroom. I hear the whoosh and gurgling and wonder whether there are places where wisdom just isn't at home, whether Ohio is one such *locus sine genio*. It then occurs to me that the gurgling might actually be coming from the brook that retreats into the bushes at the lower end of the estate. I try to imagine the house in its first incarnation, back when it was still practically empty. I clear it out before my inner eye, consider the simple lines, the horizontal moldings above the windows, the toned colors of the walls. I rip out the loosely woven brown carpet and turn off the spherical music quietly billowing from some kind of speaker, from the cassette recorder perhaps. I throw out a three-armed brass ceiling light fixture and the water fountain on the window sill, the painted white newspaper stand, the checkered sofa wedged between the desk and the shelf unit being used to file medical records and unopened telephone bills.

Make yourself comfortable, relax. Perry rubs his hands together, conjures up a piece of paper and asks me the usual questions so I can at least be sure that he's a doctor, that he's completed his medical studies in some subject or other. Have you ever been operated on? Do you sleep well? How much alcohol do you drink? Do you get up in the night to urinate? Is there a history of diabetes in your family, your parents, grandparents or siblings? Cancer? Depression?

Yes, no, yes...

How many cigarettes did you smoke a day?

I briefly mull it over, multiply it by 1.5 and say: two to three packs. I'm feeling generous. Perry gives me a sympathetic look, he probably knows what I'm up to and has likely rounded my answer back down. I tell him about my accident, that I want to be ready for any eventuality. He has, I can immediately tell, already diagnosed me with a mild anxiety disorder, probably already while on the telephone, because he believes it's unnecessary to have this kind of pre-emptive worry that something bad will happen to me again.

And how often do you think about smoking?

Every day.

How often exactly?

Every time I see a smoker, every time I smell cigarette smoke, when my neighbor steps out onto his balcony to have a break from his many children and lights up. The smoke comes into my apartment and I have the smell in my nostrils hours later. Every form of cigarette ad gives me a pang of longing, every scrunched-up, carelessly thrown away cigarette packet at a bus stop, every trod-on cigarette butt, every beautiful woman holding a cigarette between her fingers or just looking like she could be holding one. My reading chair in Columbus gives me a pang, and M.'s balcony in

Berlin, and my old Jeep because I've smoked some of the best cigarettes while driving through Kentucky or sleepy-hot prairies with the window rolled down in high summer—I smoked the brown Nat Shermans that I initially still had to buy in cartons in New York, I smoked and drove leisurely through this fruitful, truly blessed landscape and discovered lopsided barns painted bloodred from the 1860s, the horse-drawn carriages of the Amish, waving children in old-fashioned clothes the colors of Easter eggs with puffy sleeves. When I'm working I feel a compulsion, when I hold a pen between my fingers, when I'm hungry, when I've just eaten,

when I drink coffee or tea or when I'm only thinking about drinking coffee or tea. The drive up the main street to the campus takes little more than four minutes. In these four minutes I pass six shops and gas stations where I've bought cigarettes. I know the brands and the prices, on every journey I recall the fat, ringed fingers of the saleswomen who've plucked my pack from the rack above the till. Each one of these ugly shops with its red, white and blue patriotic logo and the eternal discount offers gives me a compulsion, each one gives me a faint, physical stitch when I drive by. (Yes, Fagerström, it's worst in the mornings.)

When I call a break during the syntax classes I observe how the smokers separate themselves from the nonsmokers, how the smokers—fewer and fewer each year—find each other and drift towards the door. Then I feel a pull. The richer cigarettes taste...I later write on the board, and they know, if they've been paying attention, the point I'm trying to make. It's one of those sentence beginners that under certain circumstances needs to be syntactically reanalyzed and reconsidered at the end.

The richer cigarettes taste the best.
The richer cigarettes taste the more we crave them.

Interesting, you're a linguist, Perry says.

I shouldn't have given that away, I think. Hypnosis and syntax have a lot in common. There's an entire school of hypnotherapy, neuro-linguistic programming (NLP), which is based on the results of linguistic research. It's precisely sentences like these or rather the resulting minimal hesitations lasting only a fraction of a second that Milton H. Erickson used to shake the consciousness of his clients. With sentences like these he pulled the floor out from under them at precisely the right moment. I've also read that having this knowledge can make a person hypnosis-resistant.

You know what, Perry says, I think you worry too much. You don't have to be perfect and you don't need to be prepared for every possible eventuality. Each day that you don't smoke is a good day for you. You achieve something every day. If one day, for some reason or other, you don't succeed, if you smoke one or two cigarettes, then you just have to start from the beginning. You don't have to be perfect.

Excuse me?

Look. We all make mistakes. We can't always be strong. It's like with driving. Everyone's driven through a red light. You acknowledge that you've made a mistake and you say to yourself that it won't happen again.

I look at him in disbelief, in disbelief and disgust. I'd love to jump out of my chair and leave. If only I wasn't such a polite person. What he's suggesting to me in this conversational tone goes against everything I've developed in my thinking about my years of addiction and withdrawal.

It's beyond comprehension: Did he really just say that it wouldn't be so bad if I smoked a cigarette? What's he thinking? Doesn't he realize that there can be only one possibility: for me to believe

that I'll never, never ever again even touch a cigarette? For eight months I've worked towards convincing myself that one single slipup, one single cigarette would defeat all my efforts. And I know that I couldn't just try again. The more often I slip, the harder it will be to give up. How would I stop again if I relapsed now, eight months after my last cigarette? How's that supposed to work? What's that got to do with a red light? The difference, I say, is that going through a red light doesn't give me a kick, my brain doesn't reward me for it, which is why I have no interest in repeating the experience.

Perry smiles unwisely. What am I supposed to do with this advice, I wonder, while he fumbles with his cassette recorder. What am I supposed to do with this person living in his wonderful, somewhat spoiled house and who has perhaps never smoked? Does he have other weaknesses? Does he even know what addiction is? Can he imagine how powerless I am when I get hold of even the tip of a justification? Why does this man, who makes these kinds of suggestions, specialize in smoking cessation? Does he not realize that if I were to take his suggestion to heart, I would buy a pack at the next impulse, the next opportunity, the next moment of bad temper, probably on my way back into the city? He's practically giving me carte blanche, he's taken the one thing I have in my hands to defend myself: the fear of committing an unrecoverable mistake, the fear of failing irrevocably.

He takes my cassette, uses his fingernail to try to find the end of the tear strip to open the cellophane wrapping. Give it to me, I say, when I see how clumsily he tries to do it, I've had practice. I run my thumb over the plastic film, feel the end of the strip and slide it with the light pressure of the pad of my thumb until the film falls away practically of its own accord. I've done it for years, two or three times a day, I say. And I now know that Perry, my addiction therapist, has never smoked.

Now lean back, Perry says.

How? I ask. A secret mechanism is hidden deep inside my armchair. I cling on and push against the backrest, making a flap jolt out and kick up my feet. Now I know why the armrests are so worn. I'm losing my grip and have the feeling I'm being tipped out or thrown backwards. I'm trapped. It wouldn't surprise me if two assistants in white coats came in and strapped my wrists down like in a bad Nazi torture film. Relax, says my hypnotherapist. How? I've never been so tense in my entire life — images from *Marathon Man* and *One Flew Over the Cuckoo's Nest* race through my mind. Make yourself comfortable, relax your muscles, don't fold your legs or your hands, he says. Can't he see that I don't have my legs crossed? I think, before I realize that this contradiction comes straight from hypnotism's box of tricks. He wants to take away my sense of security, security in my world. Breathe with your chest and your stomach, relax your stomach muscles, look towards the ceiling, a little farther back, a bit farther so your eyes have to strain a little. You feel how heavy your eyelids are becoming, relax, relax your scalp...your forehead...your temples...your mouth...your jaw...your chin. Breathe gently, you can feel how heavy your eyelids are getting. You know why you're here. You feel this "here," the room, everything going on around you in the room. Listen to what's going on around you in this room, in this house, maybe you can hear birds outside or music, maybe even a telephone ringing. No, I don't hear a telephone and I also know that Perry can't hear a telephone, and I know that he knows, and of course he knows that I know that he knows. We're really making progress. I don't believe that this Jay Perry, MS, can really achieve anything, and yet I can already feel my eyelids becoming heavy. Feel your feet, he says, feel their weight, it doesn't matter if you're wearing shoes or not. He can see that I'm wearing shoes, I think, and have to start over. Feel how you're being supported by the comfortable chair, feel how your weight is held and supported by the cushion, the weight of your upper body, your legs, your feet. I'm absolutely not hypnotizable, I think, especially not by an oddball Catholic who's never smoked, but I relax a little and listen, I relax every single muscle and feel how each one gets heavier and heavier, I hear the spherical music in the background and hear him counting ten...nine...eight...let yourself go, slowly, deeper, I could go down a flight of stairs, he suggests, seven...six...five, even deeper, he says, and now imagine that you have a cigarette between your fingers, you turn it and look at the lit end. Then someone takes the cigarette away from you and slowly moves away while you watch the spark, he takes a step backwards and another step backwards and the spark gets smaller and smaller, he takes another step, he's five...ten...twenty yards away from you, until you can only make out a weak glimmer, four...three...two, deeper. Feel how the comfortable chair is carrying you, how it supports and holds you, your arms, your back, your legs, you arrive, deeper and deeper, one, even deeper, now sleep.

The man who had taken away my cigarette disappears into the woods. It's night, so dark that I can't make out the contours of the trees. Sometimes I see the glimmer that disappears for seconds at a time behind the tree trunks, it flickers in a glowworm's rhythm, while the man makes his way through the undergrowth that's getting thicker and thicker. Then nothing. After one or two minutes I open my eyes. That was it, I think, it didn't work. But Perry's smiling, he leans forward and presses Eject. He puts the cassette in its case and sets it down on the table on its thin spine. I desperately have to go to the bathroom, he says, standing up and leaving again. The small brook gurgles outside. I push against the footrest with my calves, the backrest springs up, I'm flung forward.

I'd really like to keep working with you, he says when he returns. You have an incredibly low resting pulse, around forty-five.

That's from the hiking and the triathlons, I explain. Could we do a proper hypnosis next time?

Perry laughs. Take the cassette home with you. Make yourself comfortable on the sofa, relax and listen to how I spoke to you. You were completely still, you didn't move at all. I spoke directly to your unconscious for about thirty minutes. You can hypnotize yourself with this tape if you like, it's completely safe. Or you can check whether I've done a good job. Believe me, you're very susceptible to this kind of therapy.

I thank him, put the cassette in my bag and free myself from the chair with a bounce. Perry leads me to the front door. I take another look around the living room, on the window seat there's a coffee-table book with the title *The Quilts of Gee's Bend*. And as I say goodbye, I am once again surprised to have come across existences that I never thought possible and that to the best of my ability could never have imagined. And I reckon that Jay Perry, MS, is thinking practically the same thing.

In 1976, for reasons still unclear to me, I was sent off to a Catholic-Humanist boys' boarding school in the Lower Rhine region. Contact with this institution, where I would spend the following nine years, was obtained via my mother's favored orthopedist, whose own highly gifted son had boarded there. For the first two years I lived in the so-called juniorate, a two-story complex outside the gates of the old monastery that was surrounded by a trench. The juniorate was a separate structure overseen by a number of nuns, who attempted to outdo one another in meanness and viciousness and who were pedagogically completely clueless. The rules we lived under lacked any foundation, but after a time they revealed a harrowing, inward-looking logic that was intelligible only within our little world. Laws prevailed that would have made no sense on the outside, but to us children they soon seemed like laws of nature. Our whole upbringing was designed to make us humble, to strip away our dignity and beliefs. I remember that during the advent season we had to put our meager pocket money in small, colorful money boxes made of cardboard that we kept in our allotted wooden lockers. The lockers, which were built on one side of a long corridor, were checked by the nuns at night while we lay in the eight-bed dormitories. Those among us who hadn't folded their underwear properly or had put too little money in the cardboard crib were summoned the next day for an examination of conscience. Each of these nuns was trying, we soon understood, to win a merciless internal competition and pressured her own group for especially high contributions. Examinations of conscience with Sister Aleidis usually ended with us acquiescing to a punishment—we were sent to sweep or locked in a dark broom closet. We were actually released from the conversation only when we asked for this punishment and entered the closet (which incidentally never had to be locked) of our own free will. When I finally reached year eight and was allowed to cross the trench into the old monastery, I was a browbeaten, distracted boy. The educational goal of the first two years had been achieved. It was around the same time that my brother Stefan, whom I barely saw even though he, too, lived in the boarding school, first got caught smoking. I heard about it on a weekend visit home.

Stefan was fifteen and had already exhibited behavioral problems during his years at the Herder High School in Cologne. The safety officer of the Cologne Transport Office had caught him stealing one of the little red emergency hammers installed next to the windows on the tram so passengers are able to get themselves free in case of a fire. He incurred a fine as well as an incomparable scolding from our father. Maybe it was this discipline problem that made my parents finally decide to give him away, his brothers along with him. I don't know what Stefan wanted to do with the hammer. When the letter from the police landed on his desk, my father was indignant, the indicated facts had touched the fire inspector and fire protection expert in a sensitive place. It seemed to me at the time as if his coarse insults—always verbal, never physical—lasted weeks and months. Maybe they really did. Every time we had fresh hope that we were finally in the clear, we were hit with yet another wave of fury, the next fit of rage. We sat in silence in the dining nook, spooning our soup with heads bent, profoundly frightened, avoiding any eye contact. My mother gave not a word of defense for her eldest son, who cowered beside me crying with quivering legs, not trusting himself to wipe his fogged-up glasses, while my father talked himself into a rage for the hundredth time until, with a crimson head and swollen veins, he could only roar hammer, hammer, while repeatedly smacking the palm of his hand on the oak table. The crockery rattled, spit flew, and with every strike I hoped that now, now his head would finally burst, burst with anger. (The literal meanings that underlie the most common phrases and idioms affect us more immediately in childhood than later on when we've become accustomed to them and have practically forgotten their significance).

Stefan lived in House Quadrum at the boarding school, which wasn't actually a separate, free-standing building but rather a wing of the fifteenth-century Augustinian cloister. The windows of the rooms on the third floor looked out onto the cloister yard—the quad—which had served as a transitory space and the final resting place for the resident priests for more than half a millennium. The head priest of the boarding school, while quietly wandering along the mossy path one afternoon reading the breviary, fancied that he heard a bird singing, so contrary to habit looked up and discovered my brother sitting on the roof smoking with two or three of his friends. The boys were immediately and sternly ordered to their rooms, their parents were contacted, warnings and reprimands were handed down, the sentence set—the usual, completely normal boarding school routine. They could have let the matter rest; after six months no one would have spoken of it again. But things turned out differently, maybe because the subject of fire hazards came up in the conversation with the priest. My father's reaction was off the scale. The priest, a clever, wiry, almost austere mountain climber, who lost his life a little time later in a fall near Zermatt, must have accused my brother, and by extension my father, of attempted or at least negligent arson, an accusation that shook my father to his core. The roof of a centuries' old cloister is clearly not a suitable place to smoke. Nothing burns easier than a roof truss insulated with straw and clay that's been drying out for more than five hundred years. Running the risk of being caught by approaching teachers, the teenagers could have easily resorted to hiding their lit cigarettes under the tiles.

Our parents picked us up in the Range Rover for a weekend visit home and drove us to the house in Flanders. That weekend must have been so depressing, so awful that I've completely wiped the memory from my mind. But I remember the return journey on Sunday as if it were yesterday. We'd packed the car, cleaned the house from top to bottom and driven a few kilometers when my father, having once again worked himself up into a choleric fit, stopped in the middle of one of those long, unending Dutch highways lined with leaning poplars and turned off the engine. He swiveled around and screamed at my brother, who had dissolved into tears long before this: If I ever catch you smoking up there again I'll bring you down from the roof with a pickax. I'll ram a pickax in your asshole and pull you down, I'll rip you open and kill you.

My father clearly associated this scene on the roof with mountain climbing, a jump that was presumably triggered by the priest's pastime. It's also possible that my father had seen some mountain

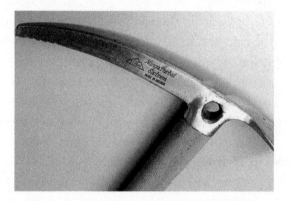

film or other during his youth, Leni Riefenstahl or Luis Trenker. He clearly meant an ice pick, which I didn't understand at the time. We were sailors, not mountaineers. In spite of this, this sentence shocked me in a way that embedded it verbatim into my memory, so that thirty years later I can vouch for its faithful reproduction. The vehemence with which this sentence and those that followed it were delivered during this twenty-minute hate speech, where the matter of this ice pick being rammed up my brother's asshole was elaborated, deeply affected and evidently, as I believe today, badly traumatized me. Though it wasn't directed at me, I have never since endured such physical fear in my life. I've never felt so trapped and at another's mercy and that my whole existence was under threat as I did then. It makes it even more remarkable that I started smoking in secret shortly after this, at least potentially exposing myself to the threatened punishment. Maybe I sensed that my brother hadn't so much breached the smoking ban as gone against my father's fire prevention rules. Perhaps I also felt that it would be harder for him to get to me. Having been given away to boarding school with relative ease at the tender age of ten, I had become completely withdrawn within the first few years. The first cigarette that I ever smoked for its own sake was a Van Nelle Halfzware rolled by a school friend we called Rosi.

In spite of my chronic-spasmodic bronchitis, my father had little interest in my attempt at conquering my addiction later on, especially in the period after I'd finished my exams and temporarily lived in his catchment area in Cologne. He would have seen how hopeless my situation was. I was the third son returned from boarding school as a heavy smoker. Perhaps he recognized that he simply had no influence over my life. After all, I hadn't been in his care since I was ten, and he barely knew anything about me and knew nothing about day-to-day life at the school, about my interests, my experiences and desires. I don't think he'd really thought through the decision to stick us in a boarding school. There wasn't really anything to think through. The damage was unforeseeable. On a rare weekend visit home when I was twelve or thirteen, I remember being accused of willful estrangement. I can only imagine how I behaved at that time: I avoided eye contact with adults, I was distant, nervous, enmeshed in my own inner world. I tried to come to terms with myself, which I managed only from one day to the next, from one hour to the next. Nothing was easy. Nothing was obvious. I didn't feel comfortable in my own skin. I blushed if someone nearby said the word "blush." Why are you so jumpy? my father asked when he laid eyes on me on our next visit home, three weeks after the incident in the car, and I knew, even though I'd never considered the concept of willful

119

estrangement before, what he meant. Are you surprised? I retorted and looked at the toes of my shoes. Are you really surprised? I would have liked to have got on the train and traveled back to the Lower Rhine to slip back into my coffin—that's what we called the small, hard crate beds—and hide under the beige-brown patchwork quilt. Many years later, my father left a message on my answering machine in which he accidently called me "sir" instead of "son." Now we're mutually estranged, I thought at the time, now you know how I feel.

There was only one reason why my father didn't meddle in my life: I was a hopeless case. He considered himself unable to help me and left me in peace with my cigarettes. Even if it sounds otherwise, I was eternally grateful at the time. Actually, there is another explanation: his sons, he would like to have thought, should be capable of developing the same willpower that he mustered up fifteen years previously. We were young men, after all, his flesh and blood. He had done it without help, now it was our turn to prove ourselves. This explanation becomes even more plausible when I recall what happened when my father got to know his second wife. She had two very pretty blond daughters who were more or less my age, maybe seventeen and nineteen years old. Both smoked, which my father would always comment on in his jovial way—he showed his best side during this period—because he didn't like it. It doesn't suit you, my father would say. The Führer wouldn't have approved, I added in my head.

One evening when the family were all together, my father offered to pay the girls not to smoke. For every smoking-free day, he would offer them five deutschmarks. I still remember how astonished my brothers and I were, how we looked at each other in disbelief. I got sixty marks pocket money a month at that time and suffered from a constant, urgent lack of funds, not least because of my cigarette consumption. I had to use this money to buy clothes, books and the train fare from the boarding school. And here we sat, five practically grown-up chain-smoking children between the ages of seventeen and twenty-two who filled the whole living room with so much smoke that the newly built oak-veneered bookcase containing our dead mother's books—her psychogram—sank into a haze, while my father, whose considerable nicotine emissions had rushed into my blood and my brain since earliest childhood, offered his girlfriend's beautiful daughters a deal (after his third bottle of Kölsch) worth 150 marks a month, which included no penalties for breach of contract. The obligation was one-sided and open-ended; they could have taken the winnings as long as it suited them. Even if they were to opt out, they would have still won on the basis that the payment evidently hadn't sufficed to keep them, who were after all German women of child-bearing age, away from cigarettes, and they could have renegotiated a new, better agreement. They were in a position to raise their exorbitant price even higher, all for the good of the master race. They could have blackmailed my father, who was interested in their success as a man of the people—an almost personal interest—and also because he wished to make a good impression on their mother. It should be noted in the interest of fairness that they didn't accept the deal. The younger later gave up of her own accord and didn't make a claim from my father. The elder is still fighting her addiction today, twenty-five years later. With an average interest rate of 4 percent, her remuneration payment from the contract has totted up to €38,293.41. Then there's the cost of the cigarettes. I would have quit then and there. I would have quit for three marks, but ultimately the proportion of men needed for the procreation of the *Volk* is far lower.

I still remember that my brothers and I smoked especially heavily that evening, with great fuss and over-the-top gestures to try to secure for ourselves a comparable contract. We thrust the packets about ostentatiously, lit each other's cigarettes from across the table and incessantly blew smoke rings. I even staged a coughing fit, one of my infamous spasmodic bronchial spasms, while my brothers clapped me on the back, but our father took no notice.

My friends and I used to smoke near a pond behind the boarding school buildings that was choked by reeds and described in the school prospectus as a lake. An overturned dinghy hull with no rigging to speak of connoted navigability. Sailing, horse-back riding, mountaineering, gliding—these were but a few of the many pastimes available to pupils according to the prospectus. Unfortunately, I never saw the mythical glider—the *Gratiaplena*—and not once in nine years did one of our guardians take the trouble to explain how we could take up the advertised pursuits. To go riding, we speculated, you'd have to bring your own horse, or win the goodwill of an especially unpleasant Latin teacher who lived next to the stables and who considered every applicant with medieval suspicion because he wanted to protect the virtue of his horse-loving daughter. Mountaineering also didn't work out, it was always the others who got to go to the cabins in Zermatt. These holiday trips were out of the question for my brothers and me as we were already tied to the house and sailboat in Flanders. We were sailors, not

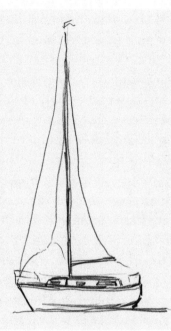

mountain climbers, our father had decided. The priest's fatal fall cemented his decision; safety was an absolute priority in our family. (My father had a four-ton sailboat built out of steel at great financial cost that could barely move but was considered unsinkable and guaranteed to be fireproof.)

As I was shut out from these pastimes and useless at team sports, I spent many years doing nothing but reading and smoking. Between the ages of thirteen and nineteen, I read and smoked absolutely everything that I could get hold of. The extent of my own boredom and mental underload back then first became apparent not too long ago when I realized that I'd read Gottfried Keller's *Green Henry*, a downright long-winded coming-of-age novel, in the 1855 and then again in the 1879 edition—a total of seventeen hundred pages filled with reflections on Goethe, antique and contemporary art, social conventions, religion, metaphysics and history. Keller leaves out nothing—absolutely nothing—of what moved the bourgeois soul of the time, while the plot could have been summarized in three pages.

I had the time, a lot of time, to read Keller and Stifter, to secretly watch the Latin teacher's daughter out riding and to go to the pond with my friends, where we smoked our hearts out. Most of the time when a teacher or a prefect got too close, we managed to flick the cigarettes into the brackish water, where they were guaranteed not to start a fire. We held our cigarettes, I've just remembered, between thumb and index finger and smoked them in the hollow of our hands right to the end until our fingertips would burn, and I now wonder if we were protecting our precious, thin cigarettes rolled with Mascotte papers from the wind—the flame would stoke up and the pleasure of smoking was diminished—or from the eyes of those in charge. (To those of you who take pleasure from the subtle observations of smoking and are interested in the ways of holding a cigarette in certain social situations, I would recommend reading J. D. Salinger's sublime *Nine Stories*, in which there is copious smoking and every mention of a cigarette, a drag, a stance or a hand movement associated with smoking has a specific function in the plot. In a few words, Salinger sketches a man on the telephone forming a peak with his cigarette ash and a shaking, traumatized soldier plucking a pack from his shirt pocket.)

We rarely crossed paths with teachers or prefects when we undertook our smoking forays during break times, afternoon free periods and on dark winter evenings. But time and time again we would bump into other packs of smokers, kindred spirits, transgressive youths in long, coarse woolen coats with upturned collars, whom we could make out far off in the distance in spite of the early falling darkness. I get flashbacks to this time when I'm in New York—where smoking's now criminalized in a way similar to how it was in the episcopal reformatory—and I pass by an office building and see the few, conspiratorial smokers huddled close together.

I'd so like to give these people, who must all have a melancholic temperament to be standing out in drafty doorways, a sign to show that I was once one of them, that I understand them. Sometimes I give them an instinctive nod to bring home my solidarity and probably end up coming across a bit strange.

I root around in my memory for my earliest experiences of smoking, and what comes to me first aren't cigarette brands or my accomplices, but the places where I smoked: the small lake; a hut next to the indoor swimming pool that was reserved two

mornings a week for the nuns to exercise in; a cellar in the three-winged House Stern; a bench below Heinrich-Böll-Platz in Cologne where you'd be shaken by every crawling train crossing the Hohenzollern Bridge towards the Central Station; a sheltered corner behind an American high school; a room with a view of the powerful volcano Mount St. Helens (it was still puffing smoke back then); a bar in the Dutch border town of Siebengewald; the mansard house in Flanders; the inner courtyard of a villa in La Jolla, California; the harbor in Alexandria, spoiled by the gigantic concrete blocks leftover from wartime; the Zócalo in the old town of Acapulco; the German Department's reference library at Bonn University.

Sometimes I imagine there's an overlay or function on Google Maps that would show me all the places I've ever smoked—a tiny black flag for every cigarette, or a blue one for every self-rolled Van Nelle that I smuggled over the border into the boarding school; an orange one for the Finas, the flat, oval, oriental cigarettes that I have to thank for some of my best literary ideas; and a red one for the filterless Pall Mall cigarettes I bought before my first flight to America in the summer of 1982. As the flight attendant handed me the sealed bag for customs, the last doubt that I had managed the passage into adulthood was erased. I spent my first American night in a tiny room in the Vanderbilt YMCA on 47th Street. I turned on the fan because the window was welded shut and the geriatric, rattling air conditioner was overworked. I lay down fully clothed on the far too short steel-tube bed, lit one cigarette after another and stared at the small television affixed to the ceiling. I noticed too late that the fan had been blowing the ash out of the shallow tin dish I had balanced on my chest. I smoked until I felt sick, I hadn't eaten anything since the inflight lunch. At three in the morning, after I'd given my window another shake, I opened the quadruple bolt lock of my bedroom door, released a swell of smoke into the dazzlingly lit corridor and took the ancient, jittery elevator to the lobby. The night watchman let me out. I walked through the vacated, stinking alleyways, marveled at the first graffiti I had seen since arriving, saw rats flit across the sidewalk, torn-open trash bags and steaming manhole covers. (It's possible that a few of my memories have become interwoven with Michael Jackson's *Thriller* video, which would come out a few months later.) I walked—no, I danced—down a deserted Fifth Avenue at the front of thirty or more zombies that moved like robots and seemed to be an extension—no, a reproduction—of me. I kept breaking formation and even jumped onto the roof of a parked car until I reached Central Park, where I gave a one-legged man a cigarette. *What's a dime?* I replied when he asked me for some change. I honestly didn't know. The worst thing about being an adult is feeling overwhelmed with embarrassment time and time again when we recall these moments in which we were so unbelievably clueless. The man hobbled and ranted after me for a while. For an hour, maybe longer, I walked through the gloomy, vacant park, gladdened and agitated from a mixture of jet lag and cigarettes. I later found out that in those days not even muggers would go wandering in the park at night for fear of getting attacked by other muggers, rapists, murderers and raging crack junkies half dead with thirst. Perhaps the crack junkies were afraid of the muggers and preferred to stay home that night too. Maybe I was lucky, and out of the criminals' fears of one another, a no-man's-land had opened up, a silent wasteland between the trenches, which I wandered through as if sleep-walking during a lull in combat. (The official New York statistics registered 174,833 violent crimes in 1982, including 107,842 robberies and 2,013 murders.)

I smoked the best cigarette of my life at a lake in a former gravel quarry near the Dünnwald wild boar park—a flag belongs there too. I must have just turned eighteen. I hadn't smoked for a few weeks, maybe due to lack of money, and had gone on a two-day art trip to Cologne with my school class. As soon as we got out of the bus in front of the Schnütgen Museum, I ran off and took the tram to my father's house. My mother's long-in-the-tooth steel-blue Range Rover stood in the driveway. I slipped into the house, looked in every drawer for the car keys and soon got lucky. I started the car and slowly drove in the direction of Leverkusen-Schlebusch, where the stunning Eliana—whom I'd recently fallen in love with—lived with her parents and brother. The coast wasn't clear at Eliana's house yet, so about half way there I turned left onto a narrow sand track and drove through a small patch of woodland until I reached the quarry. I got out and sat on the warm hood of the powerful car and pulled a fresh pack out of the pocket of my patched-up suede jacket. I found the lighter and lit my first ever relapse cigarette, and while I released the sumptuous smoke from my mouth and nose, my gaze wandered into the distance. Even though I'd been to the cinema only three or four times, the scene I found myself in didn't escape me. Only instead of the sublime, furrowed landscape of the American Southwest lying before me, it was the lead-gray mirror of a lake in an old quarry in North Rhine-Westphalia. Two empty, battered rowboats bobbed in the water, a wooden dock held up with narrow stilts with a tube hanging off the end into the water like the proboscis of a gigantic mosquito stuck out into the middle of the lake. I wondered what the cowboy from the cigarette ads thought about when he looked out over the bright red mesas of Arizona. What moved him, what was going on inside his head? He didn't have any memories, I'm sure of that. He probably didn't even have the capability to remember. And he didn't worry about his future, if he even had one. He existed only in this image-moment. Yes, he breathed. His breath, the two, three drags he took, were his entire existence, and the viewer vicariously partook in his experience through them. You could even hear the cinema audience inhaling when he took his first drag.

Yes, I thought, I know this first drag...I closed my eyes and felt the nicotine shoot through my veins after the long abstinence, it crackled in my brain like a thousand tiny explosions. I felt this magnificent firework, the titillation in my nerves, the rush of my first fall-back cigarette! I sat by the quarry, on my dead mother's 4×4, pulled the smoke in right to the tender, inflammation-prone tips of my lungs, the dopamine flooded my mesolimbic system, and I understood that the rush of relapsing is a very special gift—much more of a reward than what I had avoided in the weeks of deprivation, much more than just a catch-up effect. Throughout my renunciation, during the many weeks of deferral, I had saved something up and knew that an intense experience awaited me. I had earned it, after all. What I had experienced—this firework—went above and beyond; it exceeded all of my expectations. The cigarette at the quarry had a completely new quality. I understood that my attempt at abstinence was a kind of investment that would be paid back five or ten times over.

What the first cigarette, the relapse cigarette, meant to me was always the last cigarette for the writer Italo Svevo. I never understood Svevo in this respect. His alter ego, Zeno Cosini, a wealthy idler and incurable womanizer up to mischief in Trieste in the early nineteenth century, celebrated this last cigarette possibly a hundred times, so often in fact that he ended up using an abbreviation in his notes: LC. If the smoker sits down to (once again) enjoy his last cigarette, he is, according to Cosini, on the best path to conquer himself and to take the final steps towards a new life of health shaped by empowered action. It's the awareness that the new, better, purer existence lies immediately before him that bestows the smoker extraordinary pleasure, giving the last cigarette its unique, especially haunting flavor. The subject gets a similar treatment in *Blue in the Face*, a follow-up to the aforementioned film *Smoke*, which includes a few lines that would be a better motto for a self-help book than the false quote by Mark Twain. Jim Jarmusch, playing Bob, visits his friend Auggie (Harvey Keitel) in his tobacco shop to smoke his

LC with him. *This is it, man*, he says, and fumbles the last Lucky out of the soft pack. *Adios cigarettos*, Auggie replies. *I am touched that you would want to smoke your last cigarette with me.* Auggie knows how

important this moment is in his friend's life. Or could be — after all, they're both aware of the statistics. Nevertheless, they take a photo as a souvenir, you never know, maybe it'll work this time. They talk about their early smoking experiences. Hollywood's to blame for everything, Bob says, Marlon Brando and all the rest of them making smoking look so sexy. Then he voices the natural fear that not smoking after sex could be especially difficult. Auggie doesn't understand: *You're giving up sex too because you can't smoke afterwards?*

Unlike Bob and Cosini, I have never celebrated the last cigarette. I've always smoked it with a conscious disgust, in the knowledge that I'm just giving in to my inner, obviously already overcome weakness. Why am I smoking it at all? I would ask myself, this enormous endeavor, this immeasurable sacrifice awaits me anyway. I've just made a decision, the most difficult of my entire life! But doesn't the decision itself signify a victory over addiction? Of course! If I've decided to do something, I've practically done it, my resolution is the real achievement! (This is the reason it's so absurd when a smoker, like in the statistics cited earlier, announces he could quit if he only took it upon himself to make the decision to. There's no more perfidious a statement than: You just have to want it.)

So, why the last cigarette? Why should I smoke it? Why should I enjoy it like Cosini? I've already shown how strong I am! If I'm able to renounce a lifetime of any kind of smoking pleasure, every possible cigarette, if I've decided this and am sure of it, why not this one too? Why, when I've already come to terms with this resolution long ago, do I open the garbage bin in the kitchen and retrieve the half-empty packet that I had thrown away a few minutes ago? Why do I go into the street and beg for the last LC and—even though it's the absolute last LC of my life—make do with a substandard straight; a bone-dry filter cigarette, a Virginia offset with a glycerine and styrene-acrylic polymer? Why do I even toy with the idea of picking up an unfinished cigarette from the cobbled pavement outside my house? This LLC is perhaps the most important cigarette of my life, the cigarette that I'll remember in old age long after cigarettes have become illegal: I pull it out the bin, I smoke it standing up, I smoke it in haste, unwillingly, and it stinks. I don't know how many last cigarettes I've smoked in my life, but

I know that I've felt ashamed and hated myself a little when smoking every one of them.

The current—well, the only true—LC is the only one I actually enjoyed. I didn't know that it would be my last. Viewed this way, it was nothing special, it probably would have been long forgotten if I hadn't thought about it over and over again retrospectively. I was sitting with M. and a friend visiting from Munich out in front of our favorite restaurant in Berlin on a summer's evening and, after a light dinner, I tapped the last American Spirit out of the pack that I had shared with our friend. Maybe she'd forgotten her cigarettes, I can't remember; anyway, I gladly shared it with her. When we'd smoked the pack, the dinner was at an end as a matter of course. It wasn't necessary to initiate a farewell by referring in some way to all the work we had to do the following day. On the way home, M. said: I was just about to start again. I felt so left out, I had such a longing afterwards to share this pack with the both of you. Yes, I say, I can understand that. That's terrible. I'm going to stop. Right now. M., who must have sensed immediately how serious I was, smiled and nodded and didn't say a word. I thought of my father, of his incessant insinuations about weaknesses, and smiled too. When we were in the apartment, I began my familiar ritual: I threw away ashtrays and lighters and flung open the window. I removed everything that reminded me of cigarettes from my apartment and my life. When it was done, I tied up the garbage bag and took it downstairs. I was dog tired, utterly exhausted. When we turned out the light at eleven thirty, I fell straight to sleep.

The decision that ultimately allowed me to write this book, at least the final chapter, from the point of view of a victor, may have been spontaneous, but it was preceded by a long phase of decision making, or rather decision fixing: I knew that I would have to stop at some point. I had known it since the Thai girl gave me a light in the bar. On a number of occasions I'd managed not to smoke for months or even years, and I remembered very clearly how good I felt as a nonsmoker. Which is why at no point in my final, almost manic smoking phase did I believe that I would go through life as a smoker and grow old as a smoker and die—most probably through smoking—as a smoker.

My decision owed less to the fear of an early death (what, after all, is too early?) and a lot more to the immediate worry about my quality of life. I wasn't doing well. I wanted to be back out there, back in the mountains, but suffered with my shortness of breath. On top of this I couldn't forget the strange mixture of sadness, disgust and horror in the eyes of a friend while she sketched out in very few words her mother's battle with cancer and her final weeks of agony. My fear of the agony of dying has always been far greater than the fear of death itself.

It was therefore only a matter of time, I just had to get used to the resolution and find the right moment to take the plunge. In the meantime, I've come to realize why this (spontaneous) attempt was successful. First, I found the notion that M. could start smoking again because of me unbearable. It was also apparent that I would have practically no chance of quitting if she started smoking again. We would have reestablished our co-addiction and would have possibly had a long, long wait for the right time for us both to be ready for another attempt. Second, the pack had just become empty, the last cigarette had been smoked in an extremely pleasant setting, in a friendly atmosphere, in the best of Berlin's summer weather. I had smoked the LC without knowing it. I hadn't celebrated it, and that also meant that I didn't build up or inflate my addiction. In this moment and in the days that followed, I considered it less significant than it actually was, in fact I almost ignored it. (With the distance that I've won, I now do the opposite: I think about it every day, I seek out the memories, it all flashes before my eyes. I'm able to write this book only by admitting that this addiction was a dominating factor in my life. I'm able to make this admission, in turn, only because it no longer dominates me.)

The third and perhaps decisive factor has to have been the time, or rather the timing. I smoked the final cigarette without planning it, just at the right time of day—around ten o'clock in the evening. Sleep is what helps get you through the first and most difficult phase of withdrawal. If I'd smoked the last cigarette an hour earlier, the withdrawal would have kicked in before sleep, and I would have spent the night rolling to and fro in bed sweating and aching. Or I would have relapsed before sleeping, like Cosini. If I had smoked the last cigarette right before sleeping, I would have woken the next day with the feeling that I'd not yet achieved anything. But if I had invested nothing in this attempt, I would have probably not resisted the temptation of the first cigarette. If it hadn't cost me any effort, one cigarette, one day, one pack, wouldn't have mattered so much.

Last, I benefitted from experience: I'd quit smoking often enough, I knew what I had to do. M. and I had our agreement: for a long time the subject of smoking was taboo, which I felt would be for the best. In addition to this, I rearranged my habits, especially my eating habits and indulgences, and started working out again on day one. I drank tea instead of coffee and went without newspapers and alcohol for a few months. Already after three days I felt my condition improving. I breathed deeper and easier while I simultaneously raised my running speed and heartbeat step for step, and over six weeks I'd conquered two of Berlin's rubble mountains, the flak towers in Humboldthain, the parliamentary district, the Haus der Kulturen der Welt on the Spree, the Tiergarten up to the railway station, and finally the Salzufer strip and the grounds of the Charlottenburg Palace on my runs, and integrated them into my routine.

Have I succeeded? No. Because the first cigarette, the cigarette with which I smoke to break the fast, the one I end the long withdrawal with every time, always had a far greater significance for me than Cosini's beloved LC, praised endlessly by him over the course of long chapters. Maybe that's why I've always been in danger of relapsing—I know what ultimately awaits me should I fail. I know that I would be rewarded for my weakness a hundredfold. The first cigarette not only offsets the deficit, it brings back a moment in my life that made the greatest impression on me—the moment of absolute presence of mind that I experienced back then at the quarry, a brighter high informed by sharpness, clarity and mindfulness. When I smoke the first cigarette—and I always smoke it alone—it's as if I can look inside my own brain, as if I can discover every thought in its formation, every thrill in a neural pathway, every synaptic leap, every seminal feeling developing from my thoughts.

It would have been much better for my health and my wallet if I were to understand the matter of my own eternal struggle with addiction the way Zeno Cosini does. Right? Those who celebrate the last cigarette like a fetish object ultimately always have a reason to quit, as the right to have the last cigarette is earned only by those who really intend to stop. I can't enjoy a cigarette as the LC if I know that I won't see it through. Maybe it's happened once or twice that I've fallen for my own lie, but I soon lose faith in myself. Only those who believe themselves in that decisive moment can really enjoy the last cigarette as the last and best of their life. Smokers tend to be adept at deception, but self-deception seldom goes far enough for someone who isn't seriously willing to quit to indulge in this last cigarette and enjoy this last cigarette like Zeno Cosini.

Those, like me, who love the first cigarette above all others, always have a reason to start again. Naturally, you have to have quit first. But those who forgo smoking only because the first cigarette winks at them like a reward won't last long and they therefore put themselves in a position where they will relapse as soon as possible for the true reward. The first cigarette tastes better the longer the prior abstinence. Naturally, Zeno must have also started smoking again to enjoy his final cigarette. Only the first LC is not preceded by a relapse. (When we meet the somewhat mellow hero Cosini in Svevo's novel, he's already highly experienced in relapsing). It is this first LC more than any other that Cosini enjoys with the intention of conquering his addiction once and for all, and which he smokes long before the novel's action begins. He still believes in himself, maybe he's not aware of even the possibility of relapsing in this moment. In this sense this first LC is the best of his life, even if the victory that Cosini had carried out against himself (fancied he carried out) didn't have to be fought very hard. Only those who have relapsed a few times truly know how powerful their addiction is.

Cosini, the budding LC fetishist, smokes this first, supposedly singular LC and is a fighter, a champion, a true hero of freedom! He can enjoy his triumph for a while. But a few months, weeks, days later he remorsefully reaches for the fall-back cigarette. He smokes morosely and, due to his dejection, misses one of the most wonderful moments of his life. But not long after, he once again has fresh hope. He can, even though he hates himself for his weakness right now, already look forward to the next LC. He knows, as he's relapsed, that he can have it. Right now. Or tomorrow. Or in a week. Or on December 31. He just has to want it.

I wonder if people like Cosini can tell the difference when they smoke the final LC, whether they know intuitively that they will not circle back around again as they have before. Since this day at the quarry, I've always smoked the last cigarette because I could already sense that a new first one was awaiting me at some point in the future, a relapse cigarette that would surpass all other cigarettes and trigger a giddy clarity within me that had up to that point been waiting in the shadows. As much as I've always been ashamed of this last cigarette, it's also always brought me a private, tranquil joy.

The last few weeks have been frantic and exhausting. A long journey is now behind us and we're using the days before the semester starts to regain our strength. Maybe we'll drive home through Holmes County, I think. Nowhere in the world has more Amish and Mennonites than here in the north of Ohio. I read that smoking has caused a dispute between them for many centuries. One side quotes Isaiah 55:2 — *Why spend money for that which is not bread, and your labor for that which does not satisfy?* The other vaguely refers to tradition and explains that God himself created tobacco in order for man to have pleasure. Those who refuse tobacco reject God's creation. I also hear that many of these Luddite farmers cultivate tobacco with great pangs of conscience to feed their numerous children and to have their carriages repaired. Cultivating tobacco is considered highly lucrative, even though the US government removed the subsidies a long time ago. Is it possible for a pious community to produce and sell something when its consumption is a sin?

We don't drive through Holmes County. We drive from Cleveland, where we stayed the night at the Case Western Reserve University campus and saw some beautiful wall paintings by Sol LeWitt in a museum, and take the direct route to Columbus. On the freeway we resume a discussion that we've been having since we first got to know each other: Is it possible to have a work of art that consists solely of thought? In other words, is the work that is only a concept in the mind of the artist already art, or does it have to be actualized? I like to quote Musil on these occasions: What matters to me is the passionate energy of thought. Yes, M. says, and then he found a form for these thoughts, a form that's quite unruly at times, but one that he ultimately had under control. She actually wants to say to me that the essay form is undisciplined, that the book I'm working on is one big lack of discipline. M. solely writes poems, which are published in two-year intervals in exquisite Austrian editions. Over breakfast I made a final attempt to convince her of the detour through Holmes County. But she's exhausted. She suffers from jet lag worse than I do. Since when do you do research? she asked. Are you a journalist now? No, no need to worry. She's right. I can't go up

to strangers and hassle them with questions, especially not long-established farmers who fundamen-
tally reject modernity and its media because it's the
devil's work. Why should they answer my questions?
What does so-called public interest mean to them?
The grace of God is the one thing that counts. It's
best to leave them in peace.

The flight's really knocked me out, M. says.
How do you always manage to get over it? We were
on the move for eighteen hours, five of which we
spent in the Delta Terminal of John F. Kennedy airport, always in eye- and earshot of the dominating,
warlike state of affairs of the infamous Gate 23.

Last week an actor friend of mine who's a strong
smoker told me that he doesn't mind the long
flights he has to take for his work. He flies to South
Africa or Los Angeles or wherever and doesn't

think about smoking at all. It's as if his addiction is suspended, as if he's fallen out of time for eight or fourteen hours.

Not even the flight crew's urgent announcements requesting that passengers not smoke in the toilets disturb his peace, even though they constitute a truly insidious meanness, a real insolence from the perspective of the smoker. We board a plane, find our seat and stow away our jacket and hand luggage. We attend to our book (one that's got nothing to do with nicotine) or try to go to sleep before the first feed, we do everything in our power to forget for a couple of hours the unattainable cigarettes tucked away in our jacket pocket. And already we are reminded with subtle mockery, with a slight malice perceptible only to the trained ear, of these very cigarettes with the evidently fake, impudent reference to the fire regulations. As if a plane has ever gone down because of a cigarette fire! Why was fire safety not an issue back in 1982 when I smoked a pack and a half of Pall Mall from Frankfurt to JFK? Would we somehow crash, for instance, if a spark happened to fall on an economy seat? And didn't my father, the fire safety expert, used to smoke on flights? (He was once detained at Tel Aviv airport for five hours. When passport control asked him what his occupation was, he said "expert in explosions.") Why don't the flight attendants say what they're really thinking? It's written all over their faces: Please get a hold of yourself! We think it's revolting that you smoke. You want to poison us with your cigarettes, you want to kill us! Every cigarette, in

fact, every intended drag is an attack on our life, on our health, on our beauty! The next pimple on my delicate flight attendant cheek will be billed to your account. You should be grateful that we're taking you at all, you haven't earned it, you have no business being here. You should be ashamed of yourself. You should be considered a murderer, a murderer is what you are! If we were to crash, at least I'd be spared the long, painful cancer battle, which you'd be responsible for, and you'd go straight to hell and get what you deserve. A tirade like this would at least be truthful and would in any case be edifying. You could learn something about the kinds of people who occupy these positions in our society, who with the least amount of effort cause the most amount of inconvenience. Instead, the passenger, who had no intention of smoking on the toilet, sits in his place and simply listens to false, condescending friendliness, a rebuke under the much too thin guise of the law. Of course, the whole thing's so depressing one would love to do nothing more than light up right then and there.

But, like I said, my friend doesn't give a damn. During the flight he's completely relaxed and doesn't think about having a couple of puffs in the bathroom, he doesn't even entertain the idea. There's no point thinking about something that's forbidden, he says. As soon as he's off the plane, however, as soon as the flight captain has sent him off with a leathery smile, the addiction, the pent-up hunger, overwhelms him. Cold sweat runs down his forehead as he totters down the gangway with weak knees. He waits shaking at the luggage carousel, at passport control. In double time he looks for the exit, any way to get outside. In front of the terminal, even if he's getting picked up, even if the driver is impatiently seesawing on his heels because he's double parked and the anti-terror police could move in at any moment, he lights a cigarette. And then another one. Only then does he take a look around, get his bearings, find himself once again in a new place. Only then does he get into the car, without apologizing to the driver, and is taken to his hotel.

For me it's the exact opposite. I've got my addiction well in hand since those days. The craving seldom overpowers me and, when it does, I know how to bypass it. But as soon as I board a plane, the old hunger ambushes me. I sit there and remember the torment I endured during my smoking days, I hear the announcements, smell the jet fuel and see the dark blue uniforms of the Delta dames, and I think of nothing but cigarettes, all the cigarettes that I've been forbidden, deprived of or talked out of. And I wonder whether it is just coincidental that this smoking ban always hurts the most when declared by one of these motherly, perky, friendly women.

After breakfast in Cleveland, we settled our bill and stepped out of the dim hotel lobby into the gleaming sun reflected in Lake Erie. A hotel porter hurried towards us. M. blinked, put on her glasses and handed him a yellow ticket she pulled out from her handbag. He immediately ran off to fetch our car. The jocks who provide this service enjoy the benefit of mixing work with pleasure: on top of earning their keep, they save themselves the monthly gym membership. They get pleasure from their work and move accordingly, with elegance and vigor.

The faster they are, the more tips they get. I understand well this combination of the pleasurable with the practical. I look for a physical challenge when doing everyday things and while working too. I'm always glad when I have an excuse to exert myself, and not just in the mountains. Since I've been able to breathe freely again, I take on many daily tasks in a sportsmanlike fashion: lugging things around and helping during house moves, cleaning the house, the long walk into the city, the food shopping. I carry furniture and boxes to the fifth floor, buy long-life milk in twelve-packs, ride my bike and walk home from work in the evenings. Sometimes I employ all of my strength and stamina just to buy a single book at the other end of the city.

This hotel porter is no jock. He runs like a boy. He vanishes behind the hotel with waving arms and an open mouth. He runs like an actor, his movements don't flow whatsoever. Anyone who's ever had the chance to compare the usual film-stomp of an American action hero with the light-footed, almost silent float of an Ethiopian long-distance runner will know what I'm talking about. The best way of capturing the difference is by imagining an old tractor (Matt Damon) and then putting a maglev train beside the tractor (Haile Gebrselassie). Of course it presents an immense challenge for an actor to emulate a natural running style.

Luckily these kinds of scenes are mostly cut up in the editing suite in such a way that it can no longer be noticed. Equally great are the difficulties film-makers seem to have with the way cigarettes are held: you can't fool me, I think to myself every time I see a smoking actor who doesn't inhale and clearly has never held a cigarette in real life. Aida Turturro, who plays Tony Soprano's sister Janice, is one such example. (I suppose murderers and former soldiers have a similar experience when they go to the cinema: How can they even bear the inaccurate bangs with the gun not kicking back?)

I smell smoke as I climb into the Jeep. Our jock, who isn't a jock, stinks of it out of every pore. For the first time, I feel something like disgust at the thought that my smell perception has been aroused by the smoke particles that this American student has pumped out of his moist, mucus-filled lungs. Something that was deep within his body is now in mine. He had drawn it in through his yellow teeth, brushed it over his coated tongue, before it slipped into my nose and my throat and arrived in my bronchi. I suddenly find it unbelievable that we humans allow this to happen. It's common knowledge that everything that in some way breaches the confines of the body is branded taboo and triggers fear, anxious agitation and a deep feeling of disgust within us. There is hardly anything that disturbs us in the same way, and nothing in society is avenged like the unlawful, violent or fraudulent penetration into another body: rape is the most unspeakable of crimes. And though everyone knows that injections don't usually hurt, there's hardly a phobia more widespread than the fear of needles and injections. We're incredibly sensitive when it comes to these matters, and justifiably so. We have a right to bodily integrity. We all determine what we absorb, what penetrates us, what we merge with. This is why we grant those who infringe these boundaries in one way or another—mothers, doctors and priests—a special place in our lives. We elevate them because we have no choice. We have to trust them. We kneel, open our mouths and receive with closed eyes.

When it comes to breathing, we don't insist upon the same integrity. When we breathe and share the same air as strangers in a small room, we barely notice that our physical borders are being breached in the worst possible way—most of the time we don't think about it at all. As long as we don't smell it or see it, it doesn't bother us. Smoke makes it apparent that something permeates us that has just escaped the body, the moist, bacteria-populated bodily orifice of a stranger.

I tip the hotel porter five dollars through the open window. I feel like I have to buy a partial indulgence for my silent abuse. It's not you, it's me, I think. Don't take it personally. We pull away. Before we turn onto the road, I take a look in the rearview mirror. There he stands already back at his post and smoking as if he'd just accomplished some mammoth task and must reward himself for his effort. He obviously sees himself on a par with a long-distance runner and coughs into the back of his hand. As I said, I've either smoked or I've done sports, I exerted myself very rarely in my smoking years, and never of my own accord. There were of course instances when I had to. Often enough I would rush with my heavy bag through the Cologne Central Station to catch the train to the boarding school. I jostled and zigzagged at a running pace through the train station hall and down the flat corridors until I reached the tenth or eleventh platform, the train stopped on the side opposite the cathedral; we rural Lower Rhine folk weren't important enough for the single-figure platforms. I ran past the sausage stand, spurned the clogged-up escalator, where people lurked like Bismarck in the picture in my history book—eternally disembarking the ship, but never making it all the way down. (It's still a mystery to me why people stand on escalators; these machines weren't installed with the intent of slowing your progress.) I took two, three steps at a time, lunged towards the train and tore open the carriage doors. When I'd finally made it, when I fell exhausted and breathing laboredly onto the pleather seats and the train had started rolling, I tasted blood. Blood. My

bronchi were bleeding, a gazillion microscopic vessel tips deep within my body, just above my heart, had burst and were releasing blood, which I then coughed up out of my body. When I think about it now, I can barely grasp it, but at the time I didn't know any different; I thought it was normal. And this blood of my youth, this taste that I dispelled by lighting up a cigarette as soon as I could breathe again, is linked to the sight of the jock. I inhaled what this young boy had just pumped out of his diseased lungs.

Of course, these taboos have drawbacks. When eating, kissing or having sex, these border breaches bring us pleasure. And smoking is naturally sometimes a stand-in for these things, at least a distraction from them. Smoking eases the wait for the gratification of actual desires. It works best when you're hungry. It works only partially for sex. When I smoked my first relapse cigarette looking out at the lake in the quarry when I was eighteen and was then finally able to drive to my first love Eliana's house, I didn't get as far as I had hoped I would and had to smoke a lot to compensate. I was disappointed to discover that Eliana hadn't invited just me, but a load of other friends, among whom were many guys older than me who wore torn jeans, opened beer bottles with lighters and drew Iggy Pop cassettes out of the pockets of their biker jackets. (I had a soft spot at the time for modernist composers like Scriabin, Berg and Webern.) The party went on until late in the night and as I fell onto Eliana's brother's bed at the crack of dawn, I knew that I could never compete with those guys. Nothing would happen. No kiss, nothing. Eliana was, and remained, unattainable.

It must have nearly been midday when she stuck her head around the door to check in on me. Well, kiddo? I had a headache, a tremendous hangover. She came in and sat on the edge of the bed. The arms of her gray dressing gown were much too long, it clearly belonged to her father. I sensed that she was naked underneath it. Her nakedness was actually within reach. Kiss me, her eyes said, push this thick swathe of toweling off my shoulder. I knew then that I wouldn't get another chance. She had slipped into the room, sat beside me on the bed and looked at me confidentially, with a slightly tilted head, stroked my damp hair off my forehead and laid the flat of her palm on my chest, reinforcing this concerned gesture by leaning slightly towards me, increasing the pressure on my chest, and if I didn't act now, if I didn't immediately draw together all of my strength, seize this opportunity and make gravity my ally, then it would all be for nothing. The chance would vanish, I would have lost. I looked at her, breathed in deeply, as deep as was possible, and my hands twitched under the bedcovers. I hoped that the Iggy Pop fans had ridden home in the night and no longer stood between me and Eliana's nakedness. I wanted to touch her and pull her into the bed with me, when I noticed at the last moment the bitter taste on my tongue, the devilish mixture of cigarettes and dark beer and stomach acid that I knew from earlier youthful excesses. I'd never been so disgusted by myself. I froze, I didn't move. Eliana, who sensed how uncomfortable I felt in my own skin, sat up, smiled almost indiscernibly and took my pack of Prince from the bedside table with a casual, swiping motion that I would recall when I had the opportunity to watch a blackjack dealer in Las Vegas, who took cards from the stack silently with a lithe repeated motion. She lit a cigarette and held it to my lips. How grateful I was for this drag, how good this beautiful woman was to me! I smoked without taking my hands out from under the bedcovers and tried to withstand her gaze. And if, as I think now, I came across like a prisoner before the execution, then I envy anyone who can relive this experience. It was quite possibly the most wonderful drag of my life. And then Eliana lead the cigarette to her own full, slightly parted lips and took a deep, sensual drag. She bent over me and released the smoke, and the shimmering blue veil that caught the first autumnal sunshine sank over my face and caressed me. A kiss, better than a kiss...her lips, where my lips had been. Her breath and the smoke that we shared...I closed my eyes and sucked it into the tips of my lungs. My first true love's kiss was smoke, nothing but smoke.

It's M. who tears me away from my thoughts. She's been playing with her iPhone and shows me a photo of a New Year's Eve firework stuck in the snow, having apparently failed to go off. She thinks it looks unbelievably sad. I ask her to send me the photo for my book. We've just arrived at the northern foothills of Columbus. Do you remember, she asks, when we sat in front of the restaurant in Berlin with Elisabeth? It was a year ago...a year to the day. We went home, it was a mild evening, and you made me make a promise. Because you didn't want to think about smoking. Because you didn't want to be caught unawares.

postscript

Light up if you feel like it. I always smoked when opening a book or tackling a new chapter after a reading break. I would sit down, flatten out the page and light a cigarette before I'd read a single sentence. I would take a slow, deep drag and only then devote myself to the text. Now you do it. Smoke one for me. I shouldn't really care if you smoke or not. But as you know: I've become a vicarious smoker.

I don't want and haven't tried to persuade you to do anything, and this is why this book is not a self-help guide. I can't help you in any case. Help yourself if you want to, or don't. Your economic debt will be covered by other people anyway.

What's it about? my friends ask when I reveal the title of my manuscript, and they immediately think of Che Guevara, Marlon Brando, Audrey Hepburn. I have no interest in servicing the corresponding associations, neither the socioromantic nor the rest. I don't care about conjuring up pictures of Hollywood stars, workmen, soldiers and smoking revolutionaries, nor am I interested in mourning a lost pipe-smoking bourgeoisie. In the great conflicts of the last century, both sides have always smoked, the commoners and the revolutionaries, the poor and the rich, the right and the left, the cleverest minds and the greatest idiots. International corporations made their real cash only when they succeeded in winning over the everyman — the dull, the bored and the disaffected — to their products. Incidentally, Hitler was anti-tobacco and a militant (ahem) nonsmoker, just like King James I, who in 1604 composed a pamphlet against the *blacke stinking fume* and who had the traitor and fantastic tobacco snuffer Sir Walter Raleigh decapitated. But I don't live in 1936 or 1604. I'm interested in the present, my present — it has my entire attention.

In my dealings with cigarettes I've learned a lot about myself. In the course of my one-year preoccupation with the subject I've recalled some formative experiences and looked for the causes and the effects within my habits of thought and action that resulted from them. Through this I made use of the fact that the relationship between things, between different actions, events or objects becomes visible simply because they are examined together; they appear before the inner eye and stand one after the other or side by side on the inner stage of the mind.

What I've told is completely my own story. I hope, nevertheless, that one or another of my reflections is universal and of use to you. Perhaps I've even succeeded in awakening and holding the interest of a few readers for whom the inner world I've laid out is completely alien, because they don't smoke and never have, through my choice of form. I foster this hope as I am less concerned with the thing itself—nicotine and cigarettes—than what is at times referred to as self-management, a term that represents the ideal of autonomic action: we want to be able to decide ourselves what we do, above all, what we do to ourselves, with our bodies, with our immediate surroundings.

It's a legitimate desire, but we have to accept that our bodies don't in fact belong to us. They are not even at our disposal. Consider paid physical work, abortion laws and social norms with regard to sexuality. The phrase "at our disposal" also inplies a kind of ownership structure for the psychological realm and from that a derivable power of disposition: we are, it's said, more or less in possession of our mental abilities. At least we have ourselves under control. But actually, under closer scrutiny, the spirit is also under complex internal and external constraints, so we can hardly speak of true autonomy. Addiction is what most clearly places this before our eyes. And dealing with addiction is what allows the first, perhaps still timid steps towards some kind of self-management.

Each one of us has an addiction. Everyone can at least imagine what it means to be affected by a simultaneously familiar and unfamiliar inner compulsion that seems to act within us as if of its own accord. This is the only reason we believe that if we are attentive enough, we can take small steps towards a different state. We examine our behavior—those automatic day-to-day actions that seem insignificant—and in the process thereby understand what causes these actions. And already we have gained more freedom. We haven't won it (the way you win the lottery), but we have taken it for ourselves. How is this possible? I learn not through my dealings with a thing, but rather through contemplating my behavior during my dealings with the thing. To contemplate something is to embed oneself into the inner experience that corresponds to a sensory impression, with an image, a scent, a sound, and then spin a thought from it, a story in which there is more than just a spark of truth.

I'm walking along a street in a cool part of Brooklyn shortly before midnight. I've forgotten where I've parked, and I've been looking for my car for a quarter of an hour. A young couple emerges from a brownstone. They go arm in arm down the few steps to the pavement. The second floor of the house is illuminated, I hear voices, laughter and the long, deep beats of Jazzmatazz. I step out from under the beam of a streetlamp and watch them. The boy is wearing a parka, the girl a much too large biker jacket with the hem of a short violet wool skirt peeping out. Her feet, tucked into white patent leather shoes, are turned in chicly. They fumble and lean in over a lighter. The girl's long sleeves protect the small, flickering flame. Their faces light up briefly, they're even younger than I thought. They straighten up and take the first drag. They reset the deficit. I close my eyes; I know what they're feeling.

These brownstones don't have balconies, that's their only flaw. Perhaps the couple left the party sooner than they wanted. Maybe they're just going around the block and will come back later. Maybe they don't care about the party and are just in love. I could keep speculating like this, but it wouldn't lead anywhere. There's only one thing I can say with any surety, because I haven't forgotten: I know that in these first few seconds, they are truly happy.

They stroll down the street and disappear into the darkness. I can still just about make out how they lightly and jokily bump into each other—

they smoke, they giggle, the girl dances and tries to fall in step with her boyfriend, and they link arms. For the first time in my life I get a sense of how much smoking is connected to youth, with love and joie de vivre. Perhaps, I think, I've just outgrown it.

I would of course light a cigarette in this moment if I were still a smoker, only so I could process the image just afforded me. As I said: I learn by insinuating myself into the inner experience that corresponds to an external event. This ability has been bound to nicotine since my early adolescence. The regress that has plagued me incessantly during my work on this text emerges. I'm attempting to free myself from my addiction through a certain mind-set, at the same time knowing that the substance I'm dependent on is necessary for this mind-set. But I no longer smoke, and I can only hope no one notices it in the book. Or rather: I no longer smoke, and I can only hope that you can see it in every single line.

That I now no longer smoke despite the fact that smoking had such a great significance for me, my work, my thinking, and that I have left behind that phase of my life (I hope) for good, I owe primarily to my reading of Moshe Feldenkrais's *The Elusive Obvious*, which I quoted from for the epigraph of this book. A virtue of Feldenkrais is his ability to allow us to realize that for every learned behavior, even the voluntary ones, there are alternatives, and that we simply need to learn them to gain our freedom. Even if we choose to continue to do what we've done up to that point anyway, we are still freer. This is valid not least for the kind of automated behavior that we consider to be unalterable if and when it troubles us. It's as valid for physical exercise—Feldenkrais was a physicist and a judo master—as it is for patterns of behavior and reactions that are so ingrained that we hardly ever notice them. It also particularly applies to the socially learned and culturally conditioned behaviors that we refer to as addiction.

You don't have to be addicted to nicotine to experience how learning itself—not the school kind of learning, but that mental flexibility, that all-embracing inquisitiveness that we can preserve into old age—can lead to greater freedom. Are you right-handed? Try to write with your left hand for a few days. You'll find that it's a lot easier than you think. And even if you have to give up your attempt for practical reasons, you'll still feel that you're already freer. You're free to appropriate an alternative pattern of behavior—or reject it. If you make progress, you'll in any case feel something like euphoria, or at least a little thrill. Do you jog? Try to pay attention while jogging to how you jog, which muscles you move and which you try to release. Maybe you could push back your shoulders and relax the muscles in your neck. Perhaps you'll change the tilt of your pelvis, like the legendary medium-distance runner Steve Prefontaine did on the advice of his even more legendary trainer Bill Bowerman. Run a lap and pay attention to how you use your neck muscles. Pay attention to your form. Pay attention to your form when you come out of the bend and hit the straightaway, when you push your shopping cart through the supermarket, when you're peeling carrots or shoveling snow. Pay attention to how you get out of your car, how you go down to your child's eye level. Attempt to do it differently one time. Just give it a try. Learn. Pay attention. Consider what you're doing and consider what alternatives are available to you.

A few years ago the *New York Times* summarized the opinions of a handful of academic experts and sports doctors who reported that it's impossible for long-distance runners and recreational joggers alike to consciously alter their automatized running style. There isn't an optimal running style, they claimed, everyone runs differently, which is apparent when professional runners cross the finish line in a variety of styles. It must have been excruciating to watch the Czech long-distance runner Emil Zátopek, who collected one world record after another at the end of the 1940s and won three gold medals within a matter of days in Helsinki in 1952 — and who always ran like a panicked, fleeing child who'd rolled over a wasps' nest with a lawnmower. According to the *New York Times*, one must resign oneself to one's shape, to one's form, to one's rollover (there are heel runners, mid-foot runners and forefoot runners), as well as to the resulting injuries. I was surprised when I read the article because it went against my long-evolving belief that we humans are flexible creatures and in the best-case scenario never stop learning right up to old age, even and especially with our changing bodies. I believed that we are able to manipulate and optimize a lot of what we consider to be unchangeable in our lives. We can relearn our whole lives long — the most fundamental body movements, the best-rehearsed, learned patterns of thinking that seem compulsive to us. We can free ourselves from most of the routines, structures and rigid processes that we consider compulsions. One example of many from the world of high-performance sports is Marion Bartoli, until recently one of the best pro tennis players in the world, who radically changed her serve before the 2009 season. Even though she had by that point hit many millions of balls and had put in years of hard work by rehearsing the same sequence of movements until it had passed into her flesh and blood, she completely rebuilt her serve from the beginning. Anyone who has ever watched a top player

training is aware of how much courage and power are required to change a serve that is ritualized to such an extent that the smallest of muscle contractions, the tiniest of gestures constitute it.

That this is also relevant for the mental realm, that we can change not only the way our minds function through altered patterns of thought and new courses of action but also even the anatomy of our brains, has been discussed in recent times under the term "neuroplasticity" and established as a scientific paradigm to compete with the partly overhauled, often rigid theories about human development and learning capabilities associated with the cognitive scientists Noam Chomsky and Marvin Minsky, and (under the heading of constructivism) Jean Piaget. The critical period and its accompanying concept—that we learn in predetermined, strictly defined (biological) periods of life in surges and phases—seems to have served its time. There are very few time frames in human life that close forever.

We can relearn, but we can't unlearn. New studies by Theodore Slotkin, who experiments with rats in his laboratory at Duke University, confirm that the consumption of nicotine during adolescence leads to permanent neurological and functional changes that can't be reversed. The changed structures are still detectable even after the (addictive) behavior has been stopped, an effect that is especially pronounced in male animals. I see two possible ways of proceeding in light of this outcome. I can resign myself to my fate and reject all responsibility for my current actions. I am not to blame. I had no chance of evading this threat due to my upbringing. And on top of this, I'm a man. My brain is how it is. I might as well light up. The alternative is: I can't reverse the damage, but I can find new ways to circumvent my addiction. I can redirect it, I can think of my desire to smoke another way. To start with, I can write about this desire.

What is addiction? What is habit? How do we bypass patterns of behavior that we never knowingly opted for? The Enlightenment philosopher Georg Christoph Lichtenberg had a concept of neurological networks and reflected upon his own brain's plasticity, its malleability. He found an apt image for that which I have attempted to narrow down and grasp here in this book. In his youth, Lichtenberg lived on an unpaved square in Darmstadt, and from his window he observed people making their way across this square. "When the weather was good, people would go as well as they could on the diagonal. When the weather was bad or the unpaved part was very marshy, people went along the two sides and not diagonally." If it had snowed in the night, there would be a fine, crooked trace in the morning composed of a few footprints. In the course of the morning, a path would form from out of this faint route, and at around midday even "very sober and wise men" who must have known that the shortest route was the diagonal, would walk across the wonkily beaten path that had been left behind by a single sleepy night watchman or a drunk laborer. If the young Lichtenberg had lived on the ground floor or had been among those who had to cross the square every day, he would never have made this observation.

If you haven't for a while, light up a cigarette. But do what you do—seeing as you've just read a book about nicotine—more attentively than usual. Observe, for example, how you handle the lighter. Are you right-handed? You most probably find it

easier and more comfortable to hold it so that the flint wheel turns counterclockwise and the flame shoots up near your index finger. This has to do with the anatomy of your thumb. When it's bent, the joint that connects your thumb to your hand goes left more flexibly than it does right. Incidentally, children who are still wary of the flame almost always do it the other way around. They hold the

lighter so that the flame appears to the left of the wheel, and because the thumb uncomfortably dodges to the right, they press against the wheel so firmly it jams.

illustrations